Taming
Oedipus

Boys & Violence: Why?

Taming

Oedipus

Boys & Violence: Play?

Taming Oedipus

Boys & Violence: Why?

Herbert Wagemaker, M.D.

with Ann Buchholz

Ponte Vedra Publishers
Ponte Vedra Beach, Florida

Taming Oedipus
Boys & Violence: Why?
by Herbert Wagemaker, M.D.

Requests for information should be addressed to:
H. Wagemaker, M.D.
Ponte Vedra Publishers
P.O. Box 773
Ponte Vedra Beach, FL 32004-0773

Library of Congress Cataloging-in-Publication Data

Copyright © 1999 by Herbert Wagemaker

Wagemaker, Herbert
Taming Oedipus/Boys & Violence: Why?
Herbert Wagemaker, M.D. with Ann Buchholz
Includes bibliographical references and index.
ISBN: 0-9654996-4-2

Some of the names in this book have been changed to protect the privacy and anonymity of the individuals described.

Edited by Ann Buchholz
Cover, book, and diagrams designed by Teresa St. John
Cover photo: Digital imagery® copyright 1999 PhotoDisc, Inc.

Printed in the United States of America

This book is dedicated to
my grandsons:

Hunter Brennick
and
Alex Riegler

real boys, becoming real men

Contents

Acknowledgments

This book comes out of a great concern about the violence that is erupting in our schools. Many reasons have been put forth to explain why this is happening: our culture, lack of school prayer, the media, guns, parenting. Although there is some truth in all of these reasons, they seem to be shallow and unsatisfying. This book is an attempt to look, perhaps, for deeper reasons for this far-reaching violence. The causes of violence and their solutions, however, are very complex.

This book also comes out of years of contact with high school students as a team physician, youth worker, coach, parent, and psychiatrist – just hanging out with kids. Young Life, as well, has graciously allowed me to work with their organization in youth ministry.

I've also learned much about young people from my wife, Mary Ann, who for many years got to know, listened to, fed, mentored, and counseled young women.

Ann Buchholz again edited a book of mine. Without her, there would be no book, or at least one that made any sense.

Teresa St. John designed the book cover and illustrations, along with readying the book for publication.

Charlie Scott, a good friend and Young Life staff member, was in on the original idea for the book, and gave me a lot of helpful suggestions for it.

Most of all, I thank the young men and women who allowed me into their worlds and never made me feel unwelcomed.

Introduction

All of us are appalled and horrified at what has been going on at our schools – kids are on a killing rampage. Luke Woodham of Pearl, Mississippi, aged 16 at the time, first killed his mom, and then went to his high school and opened fire with a gun. Two students were killed, seven wounded. Barry Loukaitis, 14, of Moses Lake, Washington, killed a teacher and two students and wounded another. Michael Carneal, 14, of West Paducah, Kentucky, shot three students to death at an early morning high school prayer meeting on December 1, 1997. Mitchell Johnson, 13, and Andrew Golden, 11, in Jonesboro, Arkansas, set off the fire alarm at their school on March 24, 1998. During the evacuation, they shot and killed four students and a teacher. Kipland (Kip) Kinkel, 15, of Springfield, Oregon, killed his parents, went to his school, and shot 24 students, killing two. On April 20, 1999, Tuesday, around 11 a.m., Eric Harris, 18, and Dylan Klebold, 17, walked into Columbine High School with revenge in mind. They carried guns and bombs to spread their litany of death. By the time they had killed themselves, one teacher and twelve students were dead, and 23 other students were wounded. And just a few weeks later, Thomas Solomon, 15, in Conyers, Georgia, wounded six students.

What in the world is going on? How did we get to this point? What are we doing wrong? How can we correct it? These are key questions with no easy answers.

In some ways, the Columbine High School shooting incident was more horrifying than the others were. Maybe it was because so many were killed. Maybe it was because there were so many warnings. Maybe it was because it finally got our attention. After all, this was a suburban school, one in an affluent

11

neighborhood near Denver. Tragedies like this just don't happen here. Maybe it is our wake-up call – that something has been going on for a long time and is finally exploding out into the open. Most of us don't like what we see, and we're looking for answers. What do we blame for these tragic explosions?

Our tolerance of violence.

Our culture is a violent one, and has been for a long time. Just ask any emergency room doctor about Friday and Saturday nights in the emergency room. Stabbings and gunshot wounds are in abundance. A war is going on, but we have tolerated the violence, because it's been contained in the inner city.

The breakdown of families.

One in every two marriages ends in a divorce. Fathers are distant figures in most of these situations. Moms by themselves often cannot control their kids, especially their sons.

Gun availability.

Anyone can buy guns and ammunition in our culture, even kids. Not only can they get guns, but also the guns they get can unload 20 rounds of ammunition in 10 seconds.

Violence in the media.

Violence is depicted in movies, television, video games, and on the Internet. Given that anyone can log on, rent a video, or go to the movies, our children experience graphic violence far too often.

Not recognizing troubled kids.

Dangerous kids are in the schools our kids attend. Other kids know who these kids are. Somehow, we must find out who these kids at risk are, get them proper treatment, and prevent them from acting out their anger.

Decline in moral values.

We have programmed meaning and purpose out of our lives. Subsequently, kids perceive that life is not worth very much anymore.

Although we see some validity in these answers, we also feel an emptiness that accompanies them – they seem too superficial and too unsatisfying. Perhaps we need to look deeper into ourselves, into our very beings, for an answer. Where are we going as a society, as a culture? Are we drifting aimlessly? Have we somehow lost our way? What's going on?

I looked again at the faces of the slain Columbine High School students – bright, energetic, full of life, with high expectations – gone, blown away. I also looked into the face of Dave Sanders, a teacher who bled to death after directing kids to safety and saving the lives of many students. His last words were, "Tell my girls I love them." This tragedy must not, cannot, happen again. We must take control and put in measures that will end this type of destruction. Our schools must be safe for our children.

There is hope, however. I think we need to look first at how we deal with boys in our culture and how we bring up our sons. Often, dads are not in the picture. Even if they are in the picture, they frequently give their sons mixed messages about being tough on the one hand and kind and considerate on the other. Sons often feel alone, cut loose from their moms at an early age and not connected to their dads. I think that whatever factors got our culture to this point are very complex. I hope that we can look at what's going on and be willing to change things in order to make us less violent. The first place we need to explore is the world in which boys live, paying attention to how they are raised.

1

The World of Boys

I think all of us would agree that it is tough to be a teenager today, in this culture. We live in the fast lane, and kids are exposed to so much more than what previous generations were exposed to.

Boys have a hard time. On the one hand, we encourage them to be tough, independent, insensitive to what's going on inside them, stoic, cool. Then, on the other hand, we want them to be sensitive, loving, vulnerable, sharing their thoughts and feelings, loving, kind. This message is contradictory, and boys are confused. They are not doing as well in school as they used to and they are not doing as well outside of school either. In his book *Real Boys*, psychologist William Pollack, Ph.D., addresses this issue. He calls this tough, independent, strong, self-reliant model of boys "boy code" and maintains that this idea of how boys should be is outmoded. Where do we get this idea anyway? It just permeates our culture. When I was young, the Saturday movies portrayed the heroes in the cowboy movies as tough, decisive men who, after catching all the bad guys, rode off into the sunset looking for another adventure. Guys like John Wayne and Humphrey Bogart showed us how to be tough, independent, and cool. Because we have this tough, independent idea about boys, we try to separate them too fast from their moms and then from their dads. Little boys are not little men, but often, we want to teach them and prepare them for the "real" world in which men live.

Brent is 15 years old. He recently started high school at a different school across town. Brent was invited to attend this special high school because he did well academically in junior high school. His mom was delighted that Brent was going to this school, but she was also worried. Brent's grades had fallen off, and he was even failing English, something he had never done before.

When anyone asked Brent how things were, he would reply, "Fine, everything is fine." He told the school counselor the same thing. His mom knew something was going on, but the more she questioned him, the more he told her that everything was fine. Still, her instinct told her that something was going on. Brent had a hard time talking to me. He did not really want to be in my office, but, because of his mom's concern, he was there. At first, he hardly looked me in the eye. After a few sessions, he became more comfortable and told me some things that were on his mind.

"My friends all went to a high school near where we live. I miss them. Some of us had been together since kindergarten, and I could count on them. I didn't know anybody at this new school, at least no one I knew very well. It's hard to make new friends. I just don't fit in."

Brent was small for his age and somewhat shy. I could see why he was having problems. His grades were falling, and for the first time in his school experience, he was having problems academically. He just couldn't get motivated and he had a hard time studying. But Brent relayed that everything was "fine."

I asked him how he was handling everything. He replied, "I find myself getting sad, but I am able to handle it. I just don't show anyone how I'm feeling."

"What do you do with this sadness?" I asked.

"I let it churn inside me. Sometimes I get so angry that I just scream. But I only do that when no one can hear me."

Brent is a frustrated kid who keeps his feelings inside. He is a lonely, sad teenager who is having a hard time adjusting to a new school. He's not telling anyone how he feels. That is, he's keeping his feelings behind a mask, a mask of masculinity that tells him to keep his feelings undercover, hidden.

Why do boys hide behind their masks of masculinity? Boys at an early age pick up that they should not express feelings. If they get hurt, they're to grin and bear it. If they're uncertain, they're not to show it. If they're lonely, they just go on. To get behind the masks that sons put on, parents have to be aware that this perception exists and be aware that something is going on, as Brent's mom did.

Many boys feel that they should handle these problems by themselves. They are not expected to reach out to their moms or dads, teachers, or counselors. This vulnerability would prove that they are not up to the task in which they find themselves. Often what is going on is not even detectable until boys get into some kind of trouble, e.g., falling grades, discipline problems at school. Sometimes, they withdraw and look sad. Parents must be sensitive to how their sons are behaving.

To get into how sons are feeling, we have to create an atmosphere that is not threatening. Brent's mom could not say to him, "Come on, you are in high school now. Grow up." She needed to say, "I've noticed lately that something seems to be bothering you. Do you want to talk about it?" Often, boys won't respond the first time that you ask them to share what they are feeling. You may have to ask again, but respect their timetable. Be available when they feel like talking.

It takes time to create a safe atmosphere of sharing. Boys feel guilt and shame when they discuss their feelings. They try to hide how very vulnerable they feel. I think that one of the ways we can help them is by sharing our own vulnerability. I call this the argument from weakness. This approach can be a very powerful argument especially when dads share their own sense of vulnerability with their sons. It is important that our sons learn that we are vulnerable and that we make mistakes and fail. By sharing our vulnerabilities, we tell them that it is okay to feel this way and talk about it.

Parents need to understand that our culture often forces sons to be something that they are not. The macho image that we were brought up with has not worked very well. Little boys have feelings – they hurt. If we want them to be sensitive, sharing, caring human beings, then we must make sure that they understand that it's okay to have feelings and it's okay to share them. As I spend time with my grandsons, I am amazed at what good hearts they have and how caring, sensitive, and loving they are. These are the qualities we need to encourage in our sons. This support goes a long way in getting behind the mask of masculinity behind which our sons retreat.

It is becoming more apparent that boys who seem to be doing well on the surface are really silently suffering inside.

Often, they are confused, isolated, and alone. Feeling disconnected from their parents, brothers and sisters, and also from
themselves, they experience a pervasive loneliness that can last
a long time. They hide behind a mask that conceals their inner
feelings, what they are going through, and how they feel. They
pick up the fact that, as boys, they have to be tough, independent, and self-sufficient. But then how do they handle their
feelings of loneliness, confusion, and sadness? This mask of
masculinity hides their feelings. Everything appears okay and
cool, but in reality, it isn't.

John was in my office. He was telling me how difficult it
was to adjust to a new school. He had moved to Florida with his
folks in the summertime, and now he was in a new school. He
was not doing very well. He missed his friends and had not
found new ones yet – it was tough. Tears welled up in his eyes
when he told me this. He felt alone, isolated, and yet he had to
be here with his family. On the outside, John was tough, cool,
independent. On the inside, however, it was a different story. I
felt John's pain. John was trying hard to live up to expectations, but inside he was a sad, lonely, eight-year-old boy.

John had reasons to feel this way. He had moved from a
place he was used to, from a school he had attended for several
years. Most importantly, now he was disconnected from a group
of friends with whom he had grown up.

We understand this disconnection and the results of it. Do
we, however, understand other disconnections in the lives of
our sons? Do we realize that we disconnect our sons from their
mothers at a very early age? We have the mistaken idea that
somehow our sons will not be tough, independent, and strong
if they have their moms connected to them too long. It is interesting how differently dads and moms treat little boys when
they fall and skin their knees. Moms will pick them up, dry
their tears, hug them, and treat the sore. Dads tend to say,
"Stop crying; that didn't hurt. Be a man." Boys get a message
at an early age to be tough and to ignore feelings.

Interesting things happen on the first day of kindergarten.
Most kids are quite eager to go to school. They have longed for
the day and can't wait to get there. Most are thrilled to get
started. They want to meet the other kids, get to know the
teacher, and say good-bye to their moms. But all children are
not like that.

Ben clung to his mom that first day of school. He didn't want her to leave. Finally, she tore herself away and headed toward the door. Ben screamed out in sheer terror, and then ran to his mom. The school nurse was called in. She told Ben's teacher and Ben's mom that parents had to be firm with boys and that boys had to learn to become independent. She insisted that their peers would call them sissies and make fun of them if they wanted their moms. Again, the "boy code": Help boys become tough and independent. Don't let them express how they feel. This is the message boys get at an early age. They understand it right away. At times, even teachers and experts convey this message.

Brian's mother sent him to camp. He was seven at the time, and she wanted him to have a chance to be by himself, away from the family for two weeks. She wanted him to have an independent adventure on his own. That Wednesday, she got a letter from Brian:

Dear Mom,

I hate camp. I don't know anyone here. The food is so bad that I threw it up. Nothing is fun. I cry all day long because I miss you so much. I know you love me, so come and get me now.

Love, Brian

In response, Brian's mom called the camp director who thought it would be best if Brian stayed to "tough it out." Brian, however, returned home the following Saturday when his mom came to visit him.

Ben and Brian were just not ready for that kind of separation from their moms. Ben probably could have handled the first days at school if his mom would have been allowed to stay until he was more comfortable with her leaving. Brian, at seven, was not ready to be away from his mom for two weeks, especially for the first time. He was just too young for this experience.

Both moms instinctively knew that their sons were in bad situations. Ben's mom wanted to stay awhile longer, to make the first few days at school easier for him. Brian's mom wanted to go up to camp and bring him home the day she got the letter. The experts advised both mothers not to follow their instincts.

Premature separation was very painful for both of these kids. These situations should have been handled differently.

Young boys are taught that staying close to their mothers is something shameful. They then break away from their moms and turn to their fathers. Yet, for some boys, their moms offer the type of nurturing, loving interaction that even the most sensitive, caring father cannot give. Thus, they find themselves separated from their mother, but not able to get what they need from their father. At a young age, a boy may feel abandoned.

This painful separation that shames a small boy is supposed to prepare him for a "healthy" masculine identity. Instead, there is a deep inner hurt that lasts a long time. This trauma profoundly affects the psychology of these boys. How does this ruptured connection feel to a little boy when he's separated from the person with whom he has spent the most time and who has cherished and admired him more than anyone else? He's lonely, filled with feelings of doubt and abandonment. Also, he feels sad and confused.

A recent poll taken of children as young as nine years old showed that only 40% of boys spent all weekend with their parents, as compared to 50% of girls who did. Ten percent of the girls sampled said that they spent few or no hours with their families on weekends, whereas 25% of boys reported that they were on their own on weekends. These statistics suggest that the schism between boys and their parents begins at an earlier age than adolescence. This experience is often traumatic for a boy at this age. The younger the boy is, the worse this experience is for him. So how can we slow down this separation that goes on between little boys and their moms?

Certainly, we need to look at the mother-son relationship in a different light. Moms don't turn little boys into sissies. Moreover, they don't make their sons dependent on them by spending time together. And moms are not slaves – they don't cater to every need their sons have. A balance in the relationship must exist. Boys should have more and more responsibility as they get older. But the warm, loving, hugging relationships with moms need to continue. Boys need to be loved, just as girls need to be loved. Sons need to be hugged, kissed, and told how much we love them.

How do we stay close and still prepare our sons for the "real world"? Moms struggle with the constant pressure to separate from their sons, to somehow help them develop a masculine identity. Yet, in their hearts, moms want to remain close. They want a warm, loving relationship with their sons. They also are expected to teach their sons to be sensitive, loving, and kind. Likewise, they have to prepare their sons for the real world where they may be teased, taunted, picked on, and shamed if they show their loving, sensitive side.

Here are some ways moms can help their sons.

Be sensitive to what is going on. Realize that there is a double standard, i.e., pressure for boys to be tough, strong, independent, and separated from their feelings, yet, at the same time, to be sensitive, loving, and kind. This way of thinking permeates our culture. It is found at school, in Cub Scouts, on little league teams, all over the place. If possible, don't let your son be shamed into this kind of pressure. Don't tolerate the "boy code" at his school, with his coach, or wherever this kind of behavior persists.

Be willing to talk about this double standard with your son. Talk openly about the "boy code" and what you don't like about it. Be open to his feelings about it. Listen to what he has to say and give him the time that it takes to talk to you. Sometimes kids do not want to talk – that is okay. Don't force them. At other times, they feel like talking. Be available and spend the time together.

Listen to your son. Have special times when he comes home from school, before he goes out to play, or at night when you tuck him into bed. Make sure he knows that you are available and that you will listen. Listening is not easy – it has to be practiced. Carl Rogers coined the term "empathetic listening" to express where we try to put ourselves emotionally into the situation about which the other person is telling us. Take the time to be an empathetic, involved listener.

Listening does not always mean that we share the other person's point of view – this thought is sometimes hard to get across to kids. Kids complain to me that their parents do not listen to them. Often this means parents do not agree with them. Parents do not have to always agree, but they do have to always listen. Also, parents need to be sensitive to the fact that kids just want them to listen. They don't always want advice, direction, or even comments. They just want parents to listen.

Get physical. Moms, be physical with your son. Hug him. Kiss him. Tell him that you love him and how special he is to you. This nurturing will not make him a sissy or overly dependent on you. As a matter of fact, just the opposite happens. When boys know that they are loved, they feel free to be independent, to make good decisions, to have direction in their lives, and to make commitments. Knowing that they are loved also allows them to mature and become the person that they were created to be, considering their gifts and personalities.

Be sensitive when your son is hurting. Pick up signs when your son is troubled, sad, or angry. Ask him what's going on. This can be a simple question, e.g., "How's school going?" or "I don't see you hanging out with Jim anymore. What's goin' on?" He may not respond to your questioning, but he will know that you are interested and available.

Allow for silence. Sometimes, boys need to be silent. Respect that need. Don't demand that they talk. Boys go through cycles of withdrawing when they just want to be left alone. They don't want to talk. Also realize that sons connect with us through action, by doing something together, such as getting in a car to go to the store, reading books together, getting him to help with supper, or doing something he likes. Remain in contact, even if it is not verbal contact. Sooner or later he will come out of his isolation and want to talk again. Make sure that you are available when that happens. Give him the time.

Spend time together. More than anything else, time matters – time spent with sons. Moms need to have special times with their sons. Families need to be together. Meals are so important. The evening meal can be a great time of sharing, a great family time. Every effort needs to be made to eat a meal together every day. This experience should be a sharing, loving, happy time. Bedtime is also important. Don't stop going in at bedtime for a last hug too early in your son's life. Bedtime is a time when boys may be more open to telling you how they feel and what's going on.

Fight to stay connected. Carve out the time. Have fun, play, and listen. Get physical. Stay involved and find out what is going on in your son's life.

In the past, society recognized the importance of the mother-son relationship. These relationships were intended to be strong and long lasting. Mothers were expected to be involved in their son's lives. For some reason, this concept has been forgotten, but it is making a comeback.

A mom is a strong influence in her son's life. She is the first person who connects with him. And she is usually the first nurturing person in her son's life. This force is powerful. Moms give their sons the feelings of security, love, and safety that they need. It makes sense to encourage this relationship. It provides the groundwork for producing many men who are mature and sensitive, men who have the courage to live out their potential as human beings.

2

Adolescence – Troubled Journey

Adolescence is a time that stretches from puberty, ages 11 or 12, to young adulthood, ages 18 to 20. It is a time that starts with hormones and ends, hopefully, with competent, mature, resourceful young adults. For many, adolescence goes through college graduation. This time is difficult for many kids, typically not a smooth transition. Adolescents have to make decisions/transitions in at least four major areas of their lives. First, they are asked to break away from their families and establish a new identity, no longer dependent on their parents. Another decision involves their field of employment, a life work, or profession. Also, they often choose a life partner during this time in their lives. Finally, they try to establish a religious, philosophical basis for their lives, something that makes sense and to which they can commit themselves. These are formidable tasks, any one of which is difficult.

During this period, tension between parents and kids exists. Kids want freedom and want to be independent. They want to be treated like adults, which they are not, and parents want to slow down the process. Parents try to keep things under control, which often produces major conflict. Our culture feels that young men should become progressively independent, establish themselves, and break away from their families.

In contrast, I feel that we force young men away from their families too early. It does not make sense to push kids out of the nest, tell them they are on their own, and then watch them make some pretty stupid mistakes without the input of their families. The task of getting through adolescence is a difficult one, with a lot of big decisions. Our sons need a supportive and loving family to succeed. Dads and moms need to remain connected to their kids during this time.

Adolescence and middle school start at about the same time, with a rush of hormones and a new set of friends. Friends are starting to be more important now, and school offers a chance at some new friends. Kids find friends along many lines. Athletes tend to hang out together. This group can include the superpopular, leadership kids, the cheerleaders, and the athletes. The computer nerds also hang together, as do the outcasts, which include kids who are not popular enough, not athletes, not student leaders, and who are not able to commit to other groups. Demarcation starts early in middle school and continues through high school. If one wants to belong, one conforms. This puts a lot of pressure on kids. It makes them do things they would not normally do. Some kids choose not to conform, but there is a price to pay for that choice – they feel like outsiders. Belonging is so important at this age that few kids can resist the pressure to join and conform.

Thus, young men, trying to establish an identity, trying to figure out who they are, are forced into conforming just to belong. And society also gives them mixed messages. On the one hand, they have to be tough, independent, strong, cool, and separated from their feelings. On the other hand, they have to be open, kind, vulnerable, sensitive to their feelings. Additionally, they are trying to separate from their families. No wonder young men are confused.

During adolescence, boys are experiencing sexual feelings for the first time. All of a sudden, they are attracted to girls and going to dances and parties. Their friends, ages 13 and 14, are already bragging about how they "score" with girls. How is a boy to act? He knows his parents have certain ideas about this topic. Some parents do not want their son involved sexually with a girl. Other parents feel that their sons can do whatever, as long as they respect the feelings of girls.

There are consequences of having sex at an early age. First is the inability to handle the emotional experience. I have yet to see any 15-, 16-, or 17-year-old kids who can handle a relationship that involves intercourse. I've seen older ones who could not handle the experience either. Girls seem to be more vulnerable in this area than boys, but boys also suffer.

In addition to the emotional traumas, there are other consequences. One deadly possibility is HIV-AIDS. Other sexually transmitted diseases are also on the rise. The dangers are much greater than the ones we faced as kids. Another consequence is pregnancy. Abortions seem to be an easy way out, but they are not so easy. Most young girls have difficulties handling this option. Boys, who get their girlfriends pregnant, are also having difficulties handling abortions.

Sexual abstinence is certainly the best option. The consequences are too great not to refrain. Yet, I see many 16-year-old kids having access to cars, especially the back seat, with no restrictions. Furthermore, kids bring their boyfriends and girlfriends home when their parents are not there – a situation just asking for trouble.

I have helped patients through the traumas of sexual transmitted diseases, pregnancies, and abortions. I have sat and cried with dads, moms, and kids – it is heartbreaking. We push kids into a real world before they are ready for it and then wonder what happened.

Boys need their dads and their moms to talk to them about sex. I remember the sex talk I got from my mom as I bounded out the door to pick up my date. "Keep your pants buttoned," she yelled.

This caught me in mid-air. "What?" I yelled.

She replied, "You heard me. Keep your pants buttoned."

I got the point – it was not ambivalent. Times have changed since then, but she was right. If you keep your pants buttoned, not much is going to happen, and neither will the consequences.

Boys are confused about their sexuality. They are attracted to girls, but how are they to act? Parents give ambivalent messages: It is all right for sons to have sex, under certain conditions, as long as they are sensitive to their girlfriend's feelings. Teachers warn boys to protect themselves by wearing a condom. And their friends encourage them, asking what's going on, if they're making out.

In my entire professional life as a physician, I have never seen anyone die from not having sex or suffer from the adverse effects of not having sex. On the other hand, I have seen people die of AIDS, almost bleed to death following a criminal abortion, be depressed after an abortion, and on and on. I think that the message given to young people should be not to have sex until they are ready for the consequences – ideally with a permanent partner in a marriage relationship. Kids in their teens are not ready to take on a sexual relationship at the ages of 15, 16, or 17 years. The message we send kids should be loud and clear, but it is not. It's often very confusing.

Once I was invited to speak at the induction of students into the National Honor Society. More than 200 kids were being inducted that night. They were there with their parents – it was a big occasion. I was asked to speak on lowering the anxiety levels in our lives. The day of the ceremony I looked all over the city for a T-shirt that read *Button Your Fly* advertising Levi® jeans. I told kids that night, "If you want to lower the anxiety levels in your life, keep your flies buttoned." The kids roared, whereas the parents sat there with their mouths opened. The point, however, was a valid one.

Our sons face a lot of pressures in the area of sexuality. We need to speak openly and often with our sons about sex. If we have remained connected with them, this usually means answering a bunch of questions. Listen and be open, but do not give ambivalent messages. Give the message that you would want your daughter's boyfriend's dad to give him.

If your son is dating, he is confronting many questions. What should I do? How far should we go? What should I tell my friends? The answers to these questions should be thought about and discussed before they are faced in the heat of the moment in the back seat of a car. It is easier to behave in a responsible manner when these questions are discussed beforehand. Kids need to think about their behavior before they get into the situation.

Drugs are another topic with which parents have problems. Often, parents use denial – not my kid; it just couldn't happen to my kid! Don't believe it. Kids have access to all kinds of drugs, especially at their schools.

The biggest drug problem in our culture is not pot, crack, or LSD. It is alcohol. Alcohol use permeates our culture. We teach our kids that it is all right to drink. Not only do we teach them that it is okay, but some parents supply the alcohol. Keg parties are held in homes with parent's knowledge. Kids are expected to celebrate graduation, proms, and winning a conference championship by drinking. How many kids end up dead from car wrecks after this kind of celebration?

Our sons need to hear the unambiguous message that alcohol is dangerous. Driving and drinking can be fatal. Alcohol disrupts families. How can we as parents be role models with respect to attitudes about alcohol? Tough question. Certainly, if our kids see us drunk and out of control after our own celebrations, they receive a message. If there is an alcohol problem in their family, then their perspective regarding alcohol is more unclear. Alcohol is not a drink for kids. It has the potential of being very dangerous. At one time in our family life, when our kids were growing up, we decided not to have it in our home. This was not a bad idea. Parents, I feel, need to be role models regarding their convictions about drugs and sex. Kids are desperate for answers in these areas, and yet, the messages we frequently send are not very clear.

Coupled with alcohol exists the problem of tobacco and cigarettes. Do we allow our sons the freedom to smoke? I don't think so, at least not at home. Fortunately, fewer kids are smoking. It is not cool anymore. Again, how are we being role models with respect to this habit? For me, it is elementary – I have seen too many patients with chronic lung disease or cancer.

Pot, LSD, cocaine, and ecstasy are drugs that parents don't talk about. How can they get control of this issue? Kids do what their friends do. If their friends smoke, then they smoke. If their friends use pot, then they use pot. Know your kid's friends. Have them over to the house. Get involved with them. Give your kids the chance to find friends in activities that tend not to be involved in drugs, e.g., church youth groups, Young Life, sports. Don't use denial. Kids give lots of clues. Be sensitive to them.

Frank was 17. His parents were concerned. Frank's grades had fallen in high school, from A's and B's to D's and F's. He was getting into a lot of trouble at school also, including skipping school and not turning in his homework. Frank hung around with a bunch of kids that were a lot like him.

During our sessions, Frank told me that he had started using pot the fall of his junior year. The occasional use progressed into weekly use, and now Frank smokes pot every day. He told me that he was not motivated much anymore. "It is hard for me to just get up and go to school. My classes are boring and my teachers too demanding. I just don't seem to see any future for me anymore."

Frank was depressed also. He needed to be on medication for his depression. I'm glad that his parents were sensitive to the fact that something was going on. Frank needed professional help.

Parents often ask why kids turn to drugs. Answers to that question include: (1) drugs are available, (2) drugs are glamorized, (3) friends do drugs, and (4) kids are depressed. I had one young man tell me that the only time he did not feel depressed was after he smoked pot.

Parents don't talk much about issues that bother their sons. For sons, it is part of breaking away. For parents, it is just difficult. Kids retreat behind their masks into their double lives, the lives they don't show their parents. Whether or not we believe it, many teenagers are involved with drugs.

- 25% of adolescents smoke cigarettes
- 10% say they drink alcohol one day a week
- 18% drink one day a month
- 25% have smoked marijuana at least once
- 12% admitted smoking during the previous month
- 56% stated they knew kids who used cocaine, heroin or LSD
- 23% of 12 year olds knew kids who had tried hard drugs

The study also pointed out that kids who smoke, drink or use marijuana – the so-called "gateway drugs" – are 17 times more likely to move on to hard drugs.

For parents, dealing with the hidden life is tough. When this disconnection is combined with drugs and alcohol, the situation worsens. Parents are often taken by surprise. Sons who at one time talked to them and were somewhat warm are now closed off. Parents wonder what is going on.

Ben is acting like this tough, cool guy who never talks about things that are really important. His mom said, "I am kept at arm's length. I feel like grabbing him by the shirt and yelling at him in a loud voice, 'Hey, what's going on. Why don't you talk to me anymore?' "

Another mom told me that her son comes in from school, dumps his books on his bed, and heads out the door. He goes to a nearby park to be with his friends. "I don't know what he is doing," she says. "I think he may be into drugs, but he's so angry that I don't even know how to approach him. When he finally gets home, he goes right to his room and shuts the door. I feel totally left out of his life."

Parents don't know how to handle this predicament. They feel hurt and rejected. They feel like giving up on the entire situation. You can't do that, however, you have to remain involved in your son's life. Sons cannot be allowed to just do as they please. They need guidance, direction, support, and limits. The risk in giving up on kids is just too great. Parents have to convey that they are there for them, but even more, they need to insist on knowing where their kids are going and with whom. Likewise, parents need to keep up on what is going on at school, which can become very confrontational. But parents need to hang in there, to be persistent and to fight to be involved. Boys need to find their identity. They need to become individuals, but they also need the support and direction a family can give them. Hang in there. The struggle is well worth it.

Even when parents support and encourage their son in his attempt to be an individual, his friends may not see things that way. Peer groups are an entirely new thing for him. They have their own rules, their own language, their own way of dressing, and their own way of thinking. Peer groups demand conformity.

"When I got to sixth grade," one boy told me, "things changed." He continued, "Kids I hung around with just the previous year, who were nice guys, had changed. They hung around in a group. By the time seventh grade rolled around, some of them started drinking, smoking, and acting cool. You know if you didn't act that way, you would end up being an outsider." Kids learn quickly that what happens within the group is not talked about at home; it just isn't cool. A lot of kids live in a hidden world, a world into which we are not allowed.

Different groups establish different codes. To violate a code renders rejection, or at least humiliation. Being cool is so important. Not being cool means being rejected, left out, and humiliated. Kids have to be on their guard at all times. They need to know the group rules and follow them, or they will not be accepted.

This code can also be dangerous. At a party the "cool" kids drink. They try to influence the non-drinking kids to drink by letting them know that if they don't, they won't be invited back. This situation is analogous to the pressures extended in the areas of sex and other drugs. Being cool and included are strong motivational factors that have a strong influence on behavior. Conformity is crucial. Parents need to know their son's friends. He is likely to be doing what his friends are doing.

Peer groups communicate very clearly what they mean by "cool" to their members. Kids know what the demands are – there are few ambiguous messages. We, as adults and parents, need to be clear in our messages to kids also. For example, we can't tell our sons one thing about sex and our daughters something else. Likewise, we can't give one message about drugs and be involved with drugs ourselves. And we can't talk on the one hand about respecting women and then be abusive in our own families. Kids are confused enough; they don't need our ambiguous messages.

Jim and Berry had been best friends since their first day in kindergarten. They had gone to elementary and middle school together. Now they were in high school, but things had changed. Jim told me, "Berry was kind of a different kid. He wasn't all that good in sports, and he was really into computers. Sometimes he wore weird clothes. He really doesn't talk much and he's super sensitive about a lot of things. When other kids give him a bad time, he doesn't know how to respond. He gets flustered and mad. One day, some kids shoved him and knocked his books on the floor. So, he went to the teacher and told her. He should have just laughed it off or punched someone. Instead, he went to the teacher. I like Berry a lot, but some of the other kids wonder why I even want to hang out with him. I still speak to Berry when I see him, but I don't hang out with him much anymore. I know the other guys would get on me if I did."

Jim lost his good friend because of his new group of friends. If he wanted to belong, he had to conform. He wasn't going to risk his place in the new group of friends he had. Berry lost also. He lost a friend and felt left out.

Boys have many faces. One face is worn at home – the one parents see. There are also other faces – one the teacher sees, one the Boy Scout leader sees, one the Sunday School teacher sees. Then there is the face that the gang of friends sees. It is not hard to understand why boys are confused. It takes a lot of strength to become one's own person. There are so many forces, so many places that demand conformity. If a boy has been brought up in a home that encourages openness, vulnerability, and caring, he soon finds out that these feelings just don't work at school. There he has to be tough, independent, and cool. If he wants to belong, he has to play the game.

It seems that no matter how a boy decides to act, he is in a no-win situation. No matter if he is the macho man or the sensitive type, someone is on his case. If he is tough, cool, and independent at home, his parents feel that he is distant and unfeeling. Just about the time he figures out how he is supposed to act with his friends at school, he finds out that acting this way doesn't work at home. Instead of being admired, he is being rebuffed, which puts him on the defensive.

On the other hand, "If you treat your teachers with respect, then the guys get on your case," Rex told me. "It's hard knowing how to act. No matter what you do, someone gets on you."

Guys are confused about how they should think and act. In a test given to 150 boys, Dr. William Pollack, Ph.D., found that boys, aged 12 to 18, embraced some of the ideas that went along with the "new masculinity." They agreed with such statements as "men and women should be given an equal chance for professional training" and "courses in home management should be as acceptable for male students as for female students." They rejected such ideas as "the husband should be the head of the family" and "it's more appropriate for a mother rather than a father to change a baby's diapers." In the past, changing diapers was considered a feminine chore. These boys seemed to be breaking out of gender stereotypes into a new model of what manhood is all about.

These same boys were tested on Pleck's traditional Male Role Attitude Scale. They supported such statements as:

"I admire a guy who is totally sure of himself."

"A man always deserves the respect of his wife and children."

"It bothers me when a guy acts like a girl."

When given a chance to tell how they really feel, adolescent boys show that they try to embrace the traditional view of males, the tough macho type, but they also want to be sensitive and caring. Consequently, boys find it hard to reconcile these concepts. They are also sensitive to the fact that different situations demand different behaviors. For instance, boys act differently at home than they do when they are with their friends. Teachers also see a different side of them, as do Boy Scout leaders and coaches. It is almost as if boys have a different identity for each situation – a different way of relating, a different behavior, and even a different way of thinking. One of the tasks of adolescence is to take all these identities – the son, the student, the athlete, and the Boy Scout – and forge them into one identity that represents who they are and makes sense to them. This task is not always a simple one.

When boys look at the lives of adults, they don't always see things that make moving into adulthood attractive. One illustration is shared by James: "My dad comes home every night late irritable and angry. We always eat late because he doesn't get home until 7:30 or so. He doesn't like his boss or his job and seems trapped in the situation. Sometimes on the weekends, he has to go to his office. Most weekends he brings work home with him. Living like that doesn't look like fun to me."

Tom experienced the loss of his father. "My dad moved out four years ago when I was ten. He and my mom just argued a lot, so they decided to get divorced. My dad tries to make time for my sister and me, but it's hard for him. He works a lot, and although I stay with him every other weekend, it's tough."

Being an adult does not seem like much fun. A lot of kids perceive adulthood as hard work, separation from one's family, loneliness, and frustration. Accordingly, they have a hard time making sense of it all. They thus struggle with their own identity, which pushes them farther away from their parents, whom they desperately need to bring some order and direction to their lives. Growing up is not the great thing that a lot of adults think it is – it's tough!

3
Knowing Kids

How do we get to know our kids? What does it take? I think understanding our kids and getting to know them are more complicated, at least in some ways, than it used to be.

As I look back on my own life, when my kids were young, I realize that medicine, medical school, internship, and residencies robbed me of my kids. Medical school was demanding. I had to study. The days in classes were long and didn't end with graduation. During internship, I was on duty every third night. Residency was not much different – long days and frequent night calls kept me away from my family. My kids were growing up, and I was away from them in training.

When does knowing kids start? We know that bonding starts very early in life – at birth, and even before then. Infants recognize their mom's and their dad's voices very early, soon after their birth. Infants react to a voice, a touch. They turn their heads and make sounds in response. Most of us know children have to be cared for, held, talked to, sung to, and played with. Moms usually are very good at this type of care. Dads are evolving in this direction.

With loving care, infants feel secure and loved in their new environment. They get a sense that the world is not such a bad place after all. They get the feeling that they are wanted, that they belong. All kids are not born into this type of environment, as we are well aware, but a lot are. Grandparents, aunts, and uncles can and often do provide this kind of care for new babies.

So, after this kind of beginning, what happens? Infants become babies; babies become toddlers; toddlers become little kids. Our children grow up. Dads are busy providing for their families, often moms are also. Life is sometimes frantic. Time is at a premium and there just is not enough of it. Harry Chapin's song, *Cats in the Cradle*, tells of a father whose son was born when he was away. The father always promised the future good time, when they could get together. Of course, that never happened. Time is so valuable. How and where we spend it is so important. It should be a top priority. Time has to be spent with our kids. When we do spend time with them, it tells them more than words can how important they are to us.

How do we prioritize our time? Often, by default, we fall into it. When I was in medical school, I didn't decide how much time I would study. If I wanted to pass tests, I had to study, and I never seemed to have enough study time. I had to concentrate on getting through one exam after another. I can remember, however, pacing the hall of our apartment every night with our daughter Robyn in my arms, while she was going to sleep. More often than not, I flipped 3 x 5 cards as I walked, trying to learn material for the next test. Fortunately, my wife Mary Ann did not have to work while I was in medical school. We lived tightly, but we got through it.

How do families decide what is important for them? What do we need as a family? Most of us complicate our lives by moving into a house that we cannot afford or buying a car that is out of our price range. We are under the illusion that bigger and better make a real difference. That is usually not the case.

My medical school experience robbed me of time with my kids and my wife, time to reflect and grow as a person, even time to exercise and keep in shape. But a good thing came out of that experience – I learned that time was very important and that our supply of it was not endless. Time became one of the most important things in my life, and I had to plan its use wisely. I could not allow myself to get pulled into things that were not a high priority. I had to plan how to use my time productively. I also had to plan time to do nothing at all. As I look back at those years when we did not have a lot of money, I sometimes get the feeling that those were the happiest years of our lives. We did not have a lot of things, including a house, and the one car we had was old. But that did not seem to matter.

How do you prioritize time? I remember during my surgical residency days, after spending $2^1/_2$ years in surgical training, deciding that I did not have 18 hours a day, that surgery demanded, to give to medicine. So I got out of surgical training. Time was not the only factor in that decision, but it was a major one.

I don't know how I would have chosen my time priorities if I had been in the corporate structure. The demands of getting ahead are so great. I do not see how dads or moms can work 60-80 hours a week and still find time for each other, their kids, and themselves. Still, that seems to be the price of getting ahead and advancing. Our society is much more complex than the one in which I grew up. We have bought into the myth that bigger is better, and that things are more important than time spent with our families.

So our kids grow up. Our families get into patterns of life. When kids are young, life is not that difficult – kids respond to and look up to their parents. Parents who get to know their young kids set the stage for future relationships. Establishing an early relationship demands time. Little boys want to be played with, taken along in the car, and roughhoused with. Little girls want to help their moms, to play with them, and to learn how to kick a soccer ball. They want time with their parents. Time and getting to know your kids just go together. We know, for instance, that reading to a small child is so important for them. Reading aloud lays a foundation that helps kids learn and also builds a relationship that has the potential of growing as kids get older. But this takes time, prioritized time. This is hard enough for a two-parent family. How does a one-parent family, usually a mom, find the time? My hat is off to these moms and also to the grandparents who spend time with kids. Parents sacrifice for their kids. They take the time they would have spent on themselves reading or developing a golf swing and invest that time in their kids. Beginning early in the lives of children, spending time develops relationships. Somehow, parents must communicate to children that they are loved and important. Time with them communicates that louder than anything else they can do.

Kids are so excited about school. They cannot wait to go. The first day is met with eager anticipation. What happens in school often reflects what happened at home before that first day of school. Most kids play school – it's natural. Adults can foster this anticipation by teaching numbers, letters, and colors. Reading to children prepares them for school. Preparation is so important. Parents demonstrate their interest in what is gong on in school even before their children go there. They want them to be ready. They communicate to their children how important school is. Essentially, parents are laying a foundation for a good school experience.

Some children have problems with leaving home or getting along with others at school. Usually, these things are worked out, but sometimes they are not. Some kids have real difficulty learning. They cannot focus on work and have problems with numbers or reading. These difficulties are usually picked up easily. Teachers recognize kids who have problems learning and who can't focus.

Parents need to be involved in their children's schools and get to know their teachers. Also, parents need to be involved with the learning process by continuing to read to their children, by having their children read to them, and by helping on projects and with homework. Parents should find out if their kids learn best by seeing or hearing things, and if they learn best by being actively involved in projects, known as kinesthetic learning. A lot of boys learn this way. Kids have individual ways of learning, and parents need to find out which way their child learns. With parental guidance and supervision, structured time for study is also important. Parents contribute greatly to their children's educational experience by supporting their teachers and schools.

Regarding public schools, most of our children will attend them. I am a product of public education; you probably are also. We need to support our schools. Many excellent teachers work in public schools. They are underpaid and overworked. They feel unappreciated and undervalued. Last spring, I went to a performance at my grandson's school. I was amazed at how wonderful it was. His music teacher told me that it is becoming harder and harder to be a public school teacher these days. Many good teachers are going into other professions. What a sad commentary! Our politicians seem reluctant to fund schools appropriately. Somehow we must support public education more effectively.

As time goes on, it becomes much more difficult to be involved with the educational process in which our kids are involved. They are trying to separate themselves from us, and this process goes on until, finally, they leave home. Their friends at school are also influencing them more and more. Over time a giant power struggle could develop in which kids feel totally dominated, and parents feel they have lost control. Thus, time spent at an early age pays big dividends later on. It is hard, but not impossible, to develop relationships with our kids when they get into middle school or high school! So start at a young age with your kids and get involved early.

Several things happen as kids get older. Their friends influence them more and they are trying to separate from their parents. Out of this process comes a double life. One life is the one kids share with parents, i.e., the life they show them. The other life is the one they live with their friends. This process is not new. I'm sure that as you look back at your own adolescence, there were many things that you did not share with your parents. You would have been horrified if they found out. The problem now, however, is that kids have the potential to get into dangerous and life-threatening things. Times have changed, and thus, we must, as parents, be aware of what is going on in our kids' lives. It is dangerous not to know.

Kids behave the same way and have the same interests that their friends do. Friends are very important to them. Parents need to know with whom their kids hang out and who their friends are. Parents have more control over this situation, than they think, especially when children are younger. Kids tend to hang with peers who are involved in their same activities, such as band or sports.

Sports have always played an important role in my life. My daughters naturally gravitated that way also. Two of them swam and the youngest one was involved in track and cross country. By being involved in these activities, they got to know other kids who also swam and ran. Their friends tended to be involved in swimming and track also.

My youngest daughter, Lori, had two friends, Jenny and Val, who ran with her. They were friends all through high school. They all would camp out at our house over weekends. I knew who my daughter's friends were and I also knew where she was. I watched these kids for four years. I saw them train and get into the discipline and demands of running. I also observed at close range what her friends were like. An open house does this. Our home was always open to our daughters and their friends.

Another benefit of sports, besides channeling time productively, is building self-esteem. It told my daughters that they were good at something. Being good at something went a long way in building a concept of self for them. It's important for kids to find something at which they are good and then go through the discipline of getting better. All kids are not good athletes, but all kids are good at something. That something needs to be discovered, worked at, and developed. Parental support and involvement goes a long way in finding and developing this activity. Furthermore, this activity provides a network of kids to whom your kids can relate and become friends with. Swimmers and runners tend to be good kids. They typically do not have a lot of time to get involved with things that are not good for them. I watched many swim meets, cross country runs, and track meets, but it was time well spent.

As friends become more important in your child's life, it becomes more significant to know where your kids find friends. Our family has always been involved with church. Sundays were spent at worship services and Sunday School. Attending church was not an option. This involvement provided a place where my kids could find friends and develop relationships. My kids were also involved in Young Life when they were in high school, which also provided good friends for them.

My kids, nevertheless, also lived double lives. They crawled out of their bedroom windows to be with their neighborhood friends at night while their parents slept. They also drank, got in trouble at school, and did other things kids do – they were not perfect kids. I wasn't altogether clueless about these things. When I was the high school football team doctor in the mid-60s, I realized that heroin and other drugs were present on the campus of Gainesville High School. I chaperoned fraternity parties at the Sigma Nu house to keep high school girls out of there. With the University of Florida nearby, Gainesville was a fast town. High school kids had lots of opportunities to get into things that would not be good for them. As a result, I had to know who my kids' friends were, because kids do the same things that their friends do. Believe it.

There were some things that we, as parents, would not let our daughters do. These things were not even up for discussion. We made rules. I know that these rules forced my daughters deeper into their hidden lives – that was expected – but I wanted them to know that there were things that we would not allow them to do. On the contrary, these days parents seem reluctant to set absolutes that govern behavior. I do not agree with this approach. Kids need to know that there are destructive courses of action. Some behavior choices in all circumstances are just bad choices. The risks are just too dangerous. Yet, I see many young people who have made bad choices in their lives continue to make bad choices. They are continuously amazed that their lives are not turning out the way in which they wanted them.

Just the other day, I had a young lady on my psych ward who was 16 and bright, but she had made bad choices. She lives with her grandparents who have no control of her. She insists on choosing for herself, but her choices are not good ones. For example, she dropped out of school. Her 21-year-old boyfriend had given her a sexually transmitted disease and had also introduced her to drugs. Bright kid, but dumb choices. Her goal now is to go to college, after she completes a correspondence course that she hopes will get her through high school.

One method I've looked at with parents and their kids is to use red, green and yellow circles. The red circles are things that kids cannot do, e.g., skip school, drink, and use drugs. The yellow circles are activities that are neither encouraged nor discouraged. The green circle contains activities that are encouraged, e.g., studying, going to church, reading good books, being involved in sports. Parents need to agree with each other on what their kids can and cannot do. They should agree on limits. If they don't agree, kids play parents against each other; they are good at this manipulation.

The other day, a dad and mom brought their 14-year-old son to my office. They were at their wit's end with their son. He was sullen, angry and oppositional. The parents thought the son was out of control. He thought that they were too invasive, too controlling, and too restrictive. The son talked about "my room, my things, mine." I reminded him that the room in which he stayed was in his parent's home and that he was a guest there. He did not like that at all. He wanted to be separated from his folks, but they resisted this idea.

How much privacy should kids have? That depends on what kind of kids they are. I'm a firm believer that parents should have access to what is going on with their kids. If a son or daughter is in trouble, then his/her room is not off limits. I can't believe parents in Littleton, Colorado, did not know that their sons were building pipe bombs and that they had guns. All they had to do was walk in their sons' rooms. Parents have lost control. Their kids run all over them. That is potentially dangerous. Parents also live in denial believing, "This can't happen to my son or to my daughter." But it can and does happen.

I am never surprised anymore at what happens. Parenting includes knowing what is going on in the lives of their kids, what is going on in school, what the teachers say, who their kids' friends are, and what their kids are involved in. This understanding and knowledge takes time. But kids today face a more dangerous world than we did. It is tough being a young person these days. They need our help. It's also tough being a parent.

So, can we know our kids? Yes, I really think so, but it takes time and involvement with them. This time must be planned and prioritized. We may have to evaluate our priorities, and contemplate how much time we spend working and playing golf, whatever. Maybe we have to decide that bigger is not better, and that time spent with our children is just more important. My grandkids have taught me a valuable lesson. They want me, my time, and my involvement. My relationship with them is more important than the house in which I live or the kind of car I drive. They have taught me things about priorities and how valuable time is. Using time wisely is a great lesson.

4

Fathers – Real Men

"Fathers are not male mothers." They relate differently to their kids than mothers do – that goes without saying. Nonetheless, fathers are very important in the lives of their children. Fathers develop their own loving style in relating to their sons, and it is enjoyable to watch it emerge. Most men want to be good fathers.

How does a father become a good father? We know about bonding, and how important it is. Bonding with dads starts early, even when the infant is in the hospital. Infants respond early to the voice and touch of a dad. They respond to being held and loved. Bonding to an infant is easy, but it takes time and the desire to do so. Some dads may feel awkward, but they can overcome that feeling quickly. What dad doesn't respond when he holds his child for the first time?

Dads tend to activate their sons with rough and tumble play. Moms have a soothing effect on their children, whereas fathers arouse emotions and enliven their sons. Playing hard is a way that dads connect with their sons. If you have ever watched this rowdiness, you can see the connecting. Dads love it, and so do their sons. Boys relate through activities, e.g., playing, going fishing, shooting some hoops, going to a football game, just doing something.

Studies show that fathers are just as responsive to their sons' clues as moms are, but dads respond in a very different way. Fathers are capable of drawing out an infant's emotional expression along a wider scale of intensity and helping their sons tolerate a wide range of people and social interactions.

When sons become older, dads increase the activity, making it more stimulating. They roll on the floor together, chase each other, laugh, and just have a great time. Both dads and sons love these experiences. Sons are engrossed by the loving, active, playful attention they receive from their fathers – it is a time of continuing attachment.

During these rough and tumble exercises, which often drive moms up a wall, sons learn how to read their dads' emotions. Is this playful or serious? Sons learn how to read their dads' facial expressions, body language, and voice tones. They also get to feel emotions of their own. Is this acting too rough or too risky? Am I going too far? As a result, sons learn how to put the brakes on and how to control their emotions.

Dads who roughhouse with their kids have a great time, and they also become connected to them. Through action, dads tell their sons that they care for them and that being together is fun and feels good. These times cause joyful, happy feelings – they're great experiences for dads and sons.

Rough play leads to emotional mastery skills. Dads test their sons' limits and stretch them emotionally. These experiences force a son to know when roughhousing has gone too far and that he can stop it. In other words, sons learn to take command of the situation before it gets out of hand. These skills of emotional mastery can be used later on to master social encounters and to handle interpersonal aggression with communication skills rather than with fighting.

Most dads feel empathy for a child; it seems to come naturally for them. Fathers want to stay closely connected to their sons. Because of the reaction some dads think that they'll receive for showing love for their sons, they hesitate in giving them this kind of attention in public. They have the mistaken idea that real men don't treat their sons this way, especially in public.

Small boys want a special relationship with their dads. They want that great, exhilarating feeling that they have when they laugh and roughhouse with them. Dads, likewise, want the same thing. They want to be able to show and coach their sons on how to control their emotions, especially their anger and aggression in difficult social situations.

Fathers and mothers who want to help their children, the next generation, to be productive, creative, and fulfilled (i.e., to become what they were created to become) are called "generative parents" by Erik Erikson. These parents invest in their kids, take time with them, love them, and play with them. Generative fathers enjoy this relationship. They enjoy being needed by their children and thrive on giving them what they need to live a fulfilling life. As a result, more fathers than ever are developing close, loving personal relationships with their kids.

In a *Newsweek* poll, 55% of men felt that parenting was more important to them than it was for their fathers. 60% felt that they do a better job than their fathers did. 70% stated that they spend more time with their kids than their fathers did. Dads are getting more and more involved with parenting. That is good news for dads and their children.

A boy whose father develops a loving, caring relationship early in life benefits from this relationship for a lifetime. This type of father-son relationship pays big dividends during adolescence. These boys are less aggressive, less competitive, and better able to express feelings of vulnerability and sadness. Sons want their fathers' attention and approval. Boys who have good relationships with their dads at an early age don't have to act out or show aggression to get their fathers' attention later on, when they are adolescents.

A group of men were studied over time. At the age of 23, men who were able to compromise and to resolve conflicts had fathers who shared in their care at the age of 5. This same group of men at the age of 30 had more empathy. At the age of 40, these men had healthier social relationships and an increased capacity for intimacy. The effect of good fathering lasts a long time.

Similar studies validated this finding. The Glueck study in the Boston area started four decades ago with 240 fathers and their sons. The study showed that fathers who were supportive of their sons' social and emotional development during their first ten years of life had boys who excelled in high school and college. When fathers continued this type of relationship through adolescence, their sons' career success was also positively influenced. It is almost impossible for fathers to be too involved with their sons. The more time the fathers stayed close to their sons, the better the boys did.

How To Love Through Doing

In the past, fathers have not been involved that much in the emotional development of their sons. Consequently, it is hard for young fathers to know how to connect to their sons, even though they want to. Their dads were not role models for them. Without a role model, fathers are unsure of how to relate to their sons, although they feel love for them.

As previously noted, fathers often connect to their sons through activities, such as a play- or work-related activity. This connection starts when boys are young, by roughhousing on the floor or by playing catch. They want their dads to play with them. I remember when my grandson was five. We went to the park to hit baseballs. While resting against the fence, he turned to me and said, "This is the kind of day I dream of." It was the kind of day I dream about also.

Later on, boys enjoy the help of their fathers in doing tasks, such as working on a school project, cleaning out a room, or working on a car. Fathers show their love and concern through action. They connect by doing things with their sons. Again, I am talking about spending time together. Even though we may not realize it, these activities mean so much to boys – just hanging out doing things, such as throwing a football, riding to the store, fixing supper on the grill. These are the times kids remember. During these times, a son may share what he is thinking or how he feels. Just hanging out together helps fathers and sons grow close to one another.

Studies with boys, aged 7 though 11 until they reached the ages of 18 through 21, show that boys who had more action-oriented events with their fathers went further in school and had fewer delinquent episodes. This connection through activity that dads have with their sons pays big dividends during adolescence. A dad is able to defuse highly charged emotional situations by just saying to his son, "Let's go out in the backyard and shoot some hoops." In this way, dads provide for their sons a flexible surface from which to bounce off. Dads can set limits and get across the limitations that are needed by putting everything on hold. This process takes a good sense of humor from time to time.

Kids need this emotional support of interacting with their dads. They need to realize that there are limits to their emotional expressions, and they need to learn how to control them.

These emotions, if left unchecked, can become dangerous. Sons need to learn how to control their emotions and put limits on them.

Team Parenting – Moms and Dads Together

Dads can indirectly relate to their sons by supporting the mom-dad relationship. Both parents working together and supporting one another best carry out parenting. We know that moms provide a lot of the nurturing that children need at an early age. Dads can learn a lot from their wives about this process. At the same time, moms need to realize that dads have ways to engage their sons. Parents need to support and complement each other. Parenting is difficult; parents must work together in this process. Dads need to be physically and emotionally present and must support moms. Particularly during their sons' difficult adolescent years, moms need the support of dads. Without this support, moms feel overwhelmed, and their sons often get out of control. Dads need to be there physically and emotionally. They need to be involved!

Problems in Fathering

Many dads who really want to get involved with parenting feel ill equipped to do so. They just don't know how. There are many reasons for this: Dads are absent; they have no time; they are not emotionally committed; they didn't learn how. Even though both parents now share many gender-oriented tasks of a few years ago, it is sometimes hard for males to cross over that gender line. Feeling awkward and out of place, many fathers find it difficult to care for their newborns and toddlers.

Absent Fathers

Many new dads grew up in homes where their fathers were off making a living or doing other things – not there for them. Moms took care of small kids. These days, many men are just not close to their own fathers. They don't feel attached to their fathers, and, consequently, they don't know how to connect with their sons. New dads can't always find a role model to show them how to relate to their sons.

How do dads learn about parenting? One thing they can do is watch how moms connect to their new babies. Most moms know how to do this naturally. Dads can also read parenting books, watch videotapes, and review articles. In addition, they can attend parenting classes. And they can discuss children's issues with male friends to get their ideas. More importantly, dads can follow their instincts. Holding their sons, hugging them, and kissing them should come naturally. Feeding and changing diapers can feel odd at first, but dads can learn these skills. Most dads recognize that parenting can be fun, and they have the urge to get involved – they need to act on these impulses.

Sometimes moms attach themselves so closely with their sons that they crowd dads out. At the same time, when dads are unsure of their parenting skills, they just back off. Dads need to break through this lack of confidence and involve themselves with the care of their sons. They must become active in the parenting process and not be turned away. Moms need to be sensitive to any insecurities also and encourage dads to take an active role in parenting.

Dads generally have other pressures on them that take up time and energy. New fathers often feel that the best way to parent is to provide things for their family. This means working hard, making more money, and climbing career ladders. Dads I know often work 60 to 70 and more hours a week. This schedule not only takes time but also energy – energy that could have been used roughhousing with their sons.

Some fathers who feel out of place at home taking care of their young sons escape into work. I see physicians work long hours with patients, while their wives and young families are home without them. It's been said that no one on his or her deathbed ever says, "I wish I had spent more time at the office." Time is our most important possession. Most moms and, for that matter, most kids would rather have dads at home with them, rather than the things that extra money can buy.

Parenting takes two parents. It's a tough job, but it also brings a lot of satisfaction. It is a joint venture. Parents need to talk about how they are parenting and what they expect from each other. It is too late when a son is 17 and out of control for a mom to say to a dad, "I wish you would have spent more time with John when he was younger. I really needed you then." Dads need to be present physically, but they also need to be around emotionally and be connected to their sons.

The other day in my office, I saw a woman who was going through a divorce. She told me, "Tim worked 60 to 70 hours a week, but when he was home, he really was not there emotionally. He never interacted with the kids. He never took them anywhere or helped with their schoolwork. In fact, he barely talked to them. Now that we are getting divorced, he never calls and never sees them."

Moms and dads need to ask each other: "How's it going with the kids?" "Do I support you enough?" "Am I around enough?" Parents also need to share their values and their priorities. Dads may be working very hard for something moms don't even value. Career goals need to be discussed. How hard does each parent want to work? Should both parents work? What are their top priorities and what is the best way to achieve them? Will they have to compromise and, if so, how? They may find out that more family time is more important than a new car or a bigger house. Simply by talking openly, parents can at least understand each other and have a chance to come to some sort of agreement. A dad may feel resentment because he is working extra hours to provide more things and no one appreciates what he is doing. A mom may feel angry because dad is away from home a lot of the time and she feels that she shoulders the parenting responsibilities by herself. In these situations, parents drift apart. Dads feel left out and moms feel abandoned.

Some fathers resist getting involved with their sons because they bought into the old boy code of the tough, independent boy who ignores his feelings. They act tough around their sons. They want their sons to be strong and independent. These fathers dread the thought that their sons will become sissies or wimps. Often these attitudes are a reflection of how they were fathered, i.e., they probably grew up under the old boy code where boys were supposed to be tough. These dads somehow feel that too much love and affection will prevent boys from becoming real men. The macho father really is a myth. Kids need dads who are emotionally, as well as physically, present and who show love for them by being involved with their lives.

The marketplace also makes it difficult for dads to be with their sons. When I was in my surgical residency, there was an attitude that if you didn't work long hours, you somehow were less than manly. Real dads worked long hours. Even now, when I am around physicians, this attitude remains. Society still demands that men work long hours – it is the pathway to corporate success and the way to make it in the "real" world.

5

The Problem of Divorce

The biggest obstacle in the relationship between dads and their sons is divorce. When dad is no longer present in the house and mom has custody of the kids, it is hard for dad to be a parent. These dads often lose contact with their kids. When I counsel couples who are contemplating divorce, I tell dads up front, "Kiss your kids good-bye." Now, I know that this is not true all the time, but it is a lot of the time. Dads generally find it difficult to remain connected to their kids when they no longer live at home.

Frank and Betty were in my office. Their marriage was falling apart. They were arguing a lot about the usual things. Frank, 33, was trying to get ahead in his law firm and was working long hours, including weekends. Betty, 32, a nurse, also worked long shifts. They lived with their son, Bill, who was 8 years old, in a new house that was bigger than they needed.

Betty told me, "Things are just going downhill fast. We never seem to have enough money, even though both of us work. I don't know which bill to ignore. We don't seem to be able to stretch our money over everything. Last month, Frank decided to buy a new car, even though we couldn't afford it, without even discussing it with me. I really blew up when I saw it parked in the garage. That's the way it's been lately. We seem to fight over everything. It's starting to affect Bill now; he knows something is going on."

Frank waited for his turn, and then told me, "Things have really broken down between us – it's just not fun anymore. Both of us work hard at our jobs, but we just don't seem to get ahead. My job is demanding, and if I'm going to be made a full

51

partner in the firm, I'm going to have to put in the time. I'm working 12 hours a day and going into the office at least one day on the weekend. I'm tired. When I come home, I think we should have some of the things that working hard should give us, but Betty sees things differently. She didn't even want to move into our new house. I'm to the point of not coming home at all – it's just not worth the continuing arguments. We've drifted apart. We live in the same house, but we sure aren't connected anymore. Although we have a son, I'm not allowed to have much of an input into how we raise him."

They were right – things had really gotten out of hand, but at least they were concerned enough to come in and talk about it. I'd heard many stories like theirs. They had gotten married after they both graduated from college. Betty worked, and Frank spent the next three years in law school. Now they were in their mid-thirties with an 8-year-old son. They had gotten through some difficult years, but then they were working together for something. Now they had a son, who changed the situation, and they had overextended themselves financially. Their marriage was heading for a divorce if something didn't change.

What happens to a son when his parents go through a divorce? Usually, he feels disconnected from his father because he is no longer living with them. Sometimes a son feels guilty, that somehow he's to blame for the divorce. He feels lonely, isolated, and sad. Even though he feels this way, he can't tell anyone. When he tries to talk to his friends about it, they usually say, "You aren't the only one, so get over it." Often, sons act out in anger. They rebel, fight, and become defiant. Others withdraw to themselves and become silent.

Divorce changes families dramatically. Now, one parent, usually the mom, has custody of the kids. The relationship between mother and son changes. Now, moms have to be dads also. Often, they have to work to support themselves and their family. Often, a mom may be so upset that she doesn't have the emotional energy to relate to her son. The relationship between father and son also changes. Dads aren't around as much and don't have as much input into how a son should behave. Boys become disconnected from their dads who may see their sons only every other weekend, if that often. Sometimes dads are turned into the bad guy – the one who disciplines, causing further conflict between father and son.

Relationships with extended families change also. The mom's family becomes more involved, whereas the dad's family becomes less involved. Family friends also change. Sometimes kids move, change schools, and are forced to find new friends. This type of disconnection is pervasive. It reaches into almost every relationship the family had.

Divorce is not rare in our culture. We need to pay close attention to this third childhood trauma (the first two being separation from moms and separation because of adolescence). The parents of 3,000 kids become separated or divorced every day in our culture. Fifty percent of all Caucasian boys live in a single-parent home, and 75% of African American boys do. These boys, according to S. H. Kaye, tend to be more aggressive, are out of school more frequently, and do not do as well in math or reading. A New Zealand study by D.M. Ferguson showed that kids of divorced parents are sexually active earlier, into drugs, and twice as likely to drop out of school.

DIVORCE

- 50% of all marriages end in divorce
- 42% of marriages in low income families end in divorce
- 73% of lowest income families are headed by a single parent, usually a mom
- 12.5 million children lived in single-parent families that earned less than $15,000/year (1996)
- Only 3 million single-parent families had income more than $30,000
- Children in single-parent homes are 3 times more likely to quit school than children in families with two parents
- Fewer teenagers are confident they will find a lifelong mate than ever before
- Marriage rates are declining: 43% over the past 4 decades
- More couples are choosing live-in arrangements or putting off getting married until later in life
- Couples who live together before marriage have a higher divorce rate than couples who do not live together before marriage

Boys react differently to divorce. Sometimes they become angry and aggressive, while at other times they become sullen and withdrawn. During this time, they need extra care and extra time. They can't "tough it out" or "get over it." They need their dads and moms to come alongside and be sympathetic and loving. Often, however, this is difficult for parents. They, too, are going through a very difficult time and don't have a lot of emotional energy. It's important, therefore, that grandparents, aunts, and uncles take the time to be with these kids and be there for them.

Boys feel shame, guilt, and vulnerability during these difficult times. Often, they feel that they are somehow to blame for the divorce. John, 10, said to me, "If only I had acted differently, maybe my parents would have stayed together. They argued a lot about me. My dad thought my mom was too easy on me and that I was a 'mama's boy.' What's going to happen to me? Will I move and have to go to a new school?" Boys feel vulnerable and powerless in the situation.

J.W. Santrach, after interviewing 45 ten-year-old boys, concluded that divorce is harder to deal with than the death of a parent. Death is more clear-cut than a divorce. The parent who dies will be missed, but the child knows that he/she will not return. Kids of a divorced couple, however, hope for years that their parents will reunite, and often work hard to bring about reconciliation. Jack, 8, told me, "I tried everything. I would get them both to come to my baseball games. I even tried to get them both to go to the movies or dinner together. Nothing worked, even on Thanksgiving Day. Then I realized it was over, and we couldn't be a family again."

Divorce is devastating for kids. It is hard for them to go through it. And it is hard for parents, especially for dads who tend to lose their kids. Somehow, as a society, we must learn how to salvage marriages, work on them, and struggle with them. Often, we buy into the myth that if we just change partners, everything will be fine and life will work out. The problem with this concept is that we bring our flawed self into the new relationship. Often, that relationship does not work out either. Relationships are hard, and it is hard to live in a relationship with one person for an extended period of time. Marriage is not for kids, especially kids who age-wise should be adults. When marriages start to falter, couples need to get help and work on the relationship.

My advice to couples is to work out their problems. Work on your marriage. If you need to, get professional help – talk to pastors, rabbis, marriage counselors, etc. Take the time you need to reconcile the relationship. For our children's sake, we must work on our marriages. The statistics are grim. For the children of baby boomers, 59% of sons will live without fathers for at least part of their childhood. In 1990, 36% of all children were living away from their fathers. Dads, unfortunately, lose track of their children three years after they move out of their homes. In 1994, sixteen million kids lived with their moms, and 40% of these children had not seen their father during the past year.

These statistics point to the fact that the most important relationship in the family is between mom and dad. Being married is difficult. We are all very different. We come into marriage without a good idea about what it really is. Many of us come from broken homes ourselves, or homes where dads were absent a lot of the time, or homes where dads were not in emotional contact with us.

The marriage relationship has to be worked on. Spouses need to talk to one another. They have so many important issues that they must face together. Some examples include: What are the top priorities for the family? How do we spend our time and money? How do we raise our kids? What rules do we have for them? Should both parents work? To what church should we belong? The amazing thing to me is that so many of these issues are decided by default. Instead of deciding what to do, we decide by not deciding.

My son-in-law and my daughter go out on a date every Saturday night. What a great idea! He also stays around the house a lot when he is not working. He does not hang out with his buddies after work. Instead he's at home working on relationships there. My wife and I, over the years, met with friends every week for an evening of sharing our lives, studying the Bible, and praying for each other. I found that we could share things in a group that we could not share by ourselves without arguing. We were forced to listen to each other. Our friends often had insights into our problems, having been there themselves. I am glad that we spent that time sharing; it helped our marriage. Couples have to carve out time to be together, no matter how difficult it is.

Ted and Pat were in my office. They had been having trouble for the past year or two in their marriage. Pat told me, "I don't know what's going on. Ted spends most of his time at work or on the golf course. When he is home, he is not involved emotionally. He is always in a bad mood and angry. He does not support me when I try to discipline the kids. He hardly relates to them at all. He is just not there."

Ted states, "I just don't have the same feelings I had for Pat when were first married. For the first few years, things worked out fine. Then we had kids. All of Pat's time is devoted to the kids. If it's not schoolwork, it's dance lessons. Over the years, we have drifted apart. Now, I don't think we can get our marriage back together again. There just isn't anything there anymore." Nothing there but two kids, Patty, 8, and Jeff, 10.

I told Ted that it is important that he and Pat work on their marriage, and that he would stand a good chance of losing contact with his kids if his family broke up. That got Ted's attention. He loved his kids and wanted to be involved in their lives. I really believe parents don't want to lose contact with their kids. Dads want to be involved.

I also tell couples that love is basically not a feeling. Sure, there are feelings involved with love, but feelings come and go. Love is more cognitive than feeling. We make up our minds to be committed to another person for the rest of our lives. This concept is hard to get across to couples. Every time you "fall out of love," you don't divorce your spouse. Feelings do come back; you can revive them. Instead of running, you need to work on your marriage.

The best thing that a father can do for his son is to love his son's mother. Simple, but not easy. In surveys taken among children, the thing they feared most was losing a parent. For many kids, this fear becomes reality. One in two marriages break up. We have somehow gotten the idea that marriage is something we can go into casually. If it does not work out and if I do not "get my needs met," then I'll just get out of it. Marriage demands a commitment over time. When kids come along, then this commitment is even more important. Kids need both parents around.

Not all the news is bad news. Dads are more interested in parenting than they used to be. They want to be involved with their kids. They want to spend the time it takes to become connected to their kids. Dads spend 30% of their time in family-oriented activities as opposed to 10% just ten years ago. Fathers are working at connecting with their sons emotionally. They realize that their sons need them, and that their relationship can bring great personal rewards.

Fathers who spend the time to develop loving relationships with their sons feel better about themselves. These fathers are giving something to the next generation. They are role modeling what being a dad is all about, and they are showing their sons what being a man is all about.

Research shows that men who take their emotional attachment to their sons seriously, who want to be around more for their sons than their fathers were for them, also bond with their wives in a new and better way. Together, they share the task of parenting, a task once considered feminine. In families where dads are present and active, there are more hugs and more play. When dads receive satisfaction out of parenting, their marriages are better, and their families are more harmonious: a win-win situation.

How can a dad connect with his son? So many factors are involved in a father-son relationship that it is hard to give simple answers. There are, however, some suggestions that will help: love your wife, relate early to your son, and stay connected.

Love Your Wife.

Remind yourself that the key relationship in the family is not between parents and kids but between husbands and wives. Work on this relationship. Talk to one another and help each other – be united. Take the time to do special things for each other. Go out on dates and get away. Realize that longevity in relationships brings happiness in families. Every day I am thankful that I can enjoy my kids and grandkids due to enduring relationships. If marriages had broken up, these family ties would not be possible. Marriage has more to do with commitment over time than feelings. As we all know, feelings come and go. Relationships last because we make commitments.

Relate Early.

When your son comes into the world, be there. Get involved early – hold him, feed him, change him, talk to him, love him. Get connected and follow your instincts. Spend time watching your son grow and develop. Be involved with his first steps. Teach him to walk. Read to him. Throw him a ball and play catch with him. Teach him how to hit a baseball, dribble a basketball, and field a grounder. Whatever he wants to do, be involved with that activity. Be physical – hug him and kiss him.

Stay Connected.

Stay attached to your son no matter what. Boys are never hurt by too much love. How you show love and affection may change over the years, but continue to share it by being involved.

Even if you are divorced, make the effort to stay involved. Take the time to show up at games, to coach if you can, and to visit his school. Be active with him – take him out to supper or to a game. If you can, connect with him every day, even quick phone calls suffice. Foremost, though, communicate that you love him and that you care.

Single dads are at great risk for losing contact with their sons. If you are single, fight to keep this separation from happening. Even though it is easier to let the relationship slide, stay involved. Your son needs you, and you need him. Do not be a prodigal father, one of the 50% of divorced fathers who see their kids once a year, or the 30% of divorced fathers who never see their sons.

Help your son relate to his mom. Sons need to stay close to their moms. Often, society separates sons from moms too early. Dads contribute to this separation by calling their young son "mama's boy" if he runs crying to his mom too often. It is all right for boys to show affection to their moms. They will not grow up to be sissies. Do not make the relationship that you have with your son competitive with the one his mom has with him. He needs you both for different reasons.

Moms need support when they discipline their sons, but they also need it at other times. Sons need hugs and kisses from their moms. Do not try to shame your son into giving these up, especially when he is not ready to do so.

Support your wife in all aspects of parenting. Get together and talk about what you are trying to do and what your goals are. Try to agree and to compromise. Kids quickly pick up differences. They are experts at dividing and conquering. Support each other.

The Argument from Weakness

Little kids see their parents as big, powerful people. This conception continues for some time. Then they notice that dads and moms make mistakes and do things wrong. What a let-down – these perfect people make mistakes. About this time, kids realize that they are not perfect themselves.

Dads need to admit that they do things wrong and that they make mistakes. This disclosure helps kids deal with their own imperfections. It tells them that their parents are not perfect, as if they had not learned that already. Little kids make mistakes – they miss grounders, strike out with the bases loaded, and spill their milk. Dads can help their sons by not holding them to unrealistic standards.

At a Little League game, the coach was really giving it to his team for losing, "You didn't want it enough," he told them. How wrong he was! They wanted to win, but they were just kids who make mistakes.

It makes good sense for dads to say, "I really blew that one and I'm sorry," when they do something wrong. We need standards, but not unrealistic ones. Kids need to hear from their dads, "You did a great job," even when the job was not so great. The idea of being perfect is not a good standard to set. We never achieve perfection and neither do our kids. They need to learn early. They also need to hear from us how very special they are.

Each child has great value, even though he cannot field a groundball, shoot a basket, or get all A's. Each child has tremendous individual worth. It is nice that our children can accomplish things, that they are talented. Their worth, though, goes beyond that. Sometimes it is hard to remember this fact. We make them feel worthy when they hit home runs or get all A's. Our compliments come during these special times of accomplishments. They need to know that they are worthy even at other times, when they are not performing or when they have not done well.

Bill was up at bat. It was the last inning and his team was behind by one run. There were also two outs. Bill had two strikes on him with teammates on second and third base. The ball came right down the middle. Bill swung. The ball dribbled toward the pitcher's box. Bill was out by a mile. Bill left the park, with his dad's arm draped over his shoulder and headed for the ice cream store – a neat way to end a ballgame. Bill's dad remembered this was just a game, that there would be others, and that he had grounded out in a similar situation when he was a kid. Love for our sons is unconditional. We love them because they exist and because they belong to us. Although it is important that they find something that they are good at, love is not based on an achievement. Love is based on the fact that they exist and that they have been entrusted to us for awhile, and that we have the privilege of being parents to them.

Develop Your Own Way of Connecting

You may feel more comfortable playing rough and tumble with your son or taking him to a football game. It may be natural for you to spend time talking with your son, listening, and hanging out. Often, our sons show us or tell us what they like to do – just do it with them. Make connections. It does not really matter what you do or how you do it. It does matter, however, that you connect and build a relationship. Make every effort you can to get and stay connected.

Real Men Are Emotional

Let your son know that you have feelings, that you can be happy and have fun. It is also important to let him know that you feel sad, that you cry and that you are vulnerable. How important it is to let our sons know that we have emotions. Let him see your tender side and let him see you hug his mom.

Do you always have to win? Are you always tough? Are you always the invincible father? That's not how it really is in life. As men, we are vulnerable, e.g., by making mistakes, by doing dumb things, by failing, by crying. Showing our sons this vulnerability helps them sort out their own feelings and teaches them how to deal with these feelings.

Dads are role models. They may not be very good, but they are role models. Fathers demonstrate what it means to be a man – what being a husband and father is all about. They show their sons how to act with women and how a family operates. Being a parent is an awesome responsibility. Having kids is a different ballgame, a game in which real men are involved. It's time men become real men.

6

Invading an Adolescent Subculture

In the 1960s, my wife and I moved to Gainesville, Florida. I was furthering my medical education at the time. I became the football team doctor, which meant that I sat on the sidelines of every game and showed up at practice when I could. I came into contact with football players, cheerleaders, band members, and other kids who just showed up at the games. This position afforded me the opportunity to get to know high school students. Hanging out at football games was an easy way to get acquainted with them. My wife, Mary Ann, also started showing up at the games.

As time went on, I began eating lunch at school. Often, I felt uncomfortable in a crowded lunchroom not seeing anyone I knew. In addition, Mary Ann and I attended dances and other activities at school. We really wanted to invade an adolescent subculture to get to know these young people at a different level. Although our mission took time, it was not that hard – these kids were the greatest. After all these years, we are still involved with some of them.

Right from the start, kids were friendly. Soon, they just expected us to be around (I knew that when they stopped calling me "sir"). During the first six months, I just hung out at school. I listened a lot, ate the high school cafeteria food, and saw numerous football games. Eventually, relationships formed. I spent a lot of time with these kids because my medical office was right across the street from the school.

At that time in Gainesville, a lot of things were happening. For example, integration was just beginning. Moreover, the University of Florida was there. Kids had access to drugs and alcohol. It was also a hot bed of social unrest at the time. High school kids were exposed to many things very early in their adolescent lives. It was hard growing up as a teenager in Gainesville, Florida, during that period.

In 1965, after a few months of hanging out with kids, we started a Young Life club at Gainesville High School. As we met weekly in homes, our club grew from 30 kids to more than 100. Young Life is a Christian organization that reaches out to teenagers and presents Christianity to them in a way that they can understand and relate to. Some of the kids with whom I met and developed a close relationship never came to a Young Life meeting and never got involved with us in Young Life. Time was spent with them and relationships were made anyway. We really wanted to get to know kids and make ourselves available to them.

I remember one afternoon, after seeing my last patient, discovering two teenagers in my waiting room. Don and Jean wanted to say good-bye because they were headed to Georgia to get married. After talking for an hour or so, they realized that this rash decision was not such a red-hot idea. Kids often opened up to us. They just needed an adult to talk to. For example, Jack needed to talk about his mom who had cancer and faced surgery the next week. Joan's parents were getting a divorce. Frank was on the verge of getting kicked out of school. Brent and a bunch of his friends were stealing cars, driving them around for a few hours and then just leaving them. These kids had problems, and slowly they opened up to us.

Small groups of teenagers got together every week for a Bible study and to share their lives. We formed these small groups, six or eight kids, with a leader, and they would discuss what was on their minds and what bothered them. They talked about their relationship with their parents, how they were doing in school, problems with boyfriends or girlfriends – whatever was on their minds. I was amazed at what was shared during these meetings. Boys and girls got to know each other on a different level. They became good friends. It was interesting to see how protective guys became of girls as these meetings progressed. Attitudes really changed. An atmosphere of acceptance and respect resulted. Just taking the time to know another person and just listening opened up many doors. Even around school, these kids hung out together and became good friends.

Is this type of involvement possible today? Can we access high schools the way we did? Yes, at least to some extent. If you are invited, you can have a meal in the lunchroom with a student. I know that most schools would welcome adults who would tutor students who are having difficulty with their studies. Being a doctor helped me have access to students. Teams still need physicians. Getting involved in a high school is easy: volunteer in the drama or musical productions, show up at games or practices, chaperone dances or parties, or find out where kids hang out after games.

I think that adults can still invade an adolescent subculture and establish relationships with teenagers. These relationships can become the stabilizing force in a kid's life. Just because a young person comes from an intact family, one that does things together, does not mean that the kids have it all together. Often, they do not. Teenagers need stable adults in their lives to help them get through these adolescent years. They need parents, coaches, teachers, scout leaders, Sunday School teachers, aunts, uncles, grandparents – every adult who will take the time to listen and be there for them. Although it was hard getting so involved with those kids in the 1960s, it was probably one of the most rewarding things I have ever done.

7

Helping Your Child Make It Through Adolescence

How can we help our sons through adolescence? Adolescence is not just a time of trouble; it is also one of gratification. It can be fun seeing kids grow up and develop. It can be fun to be around young people who have so much energy. They bring an excitement to our lives that nothing else can.

Being connected is the most important thing we can do as parents. Although this principle sounds simple, it isn't that easy, especially with all the forces that try to prevent its practice. Being connected is not a passive accomplishment – you have to be actively involved, sometimes aggressively involved. Remaining connected demands time, effort, and hard work. Kids do have realistic concerns and problems. Involvement takes making sacrifices and rethinking some myths of adolescence, but it must become a top priority. Even though adolescence is a time of separation from parents, kids need the direction and support that parents and other adults can give. Kids not only need direction, but they want it and look for it. Involvement in another person's life is an awesome privilege. How great to be involved in the lives of our kids!

What is the most important thing that parents can do to maintain connection with their kids? For dads, it is to love and respect their son's mom. For moms, it is to love and respect their son's dad. Marriage is a difficult relationship, the hardest relationship in which we will ever be involved. Kids make it even harder. Relationships take time. A generation ago, divorce was not an option. Marriage relationships were difficult then also, but our parents and grandparents seemed to be more determined to work things out than we are.

Couples obviously need help. Fifty percent of all marriages end in divorce. None of us started our marriages with that intent, but often we view marriage as temporary, something that we can end if things do not seem to work out. I think it would be better if divorce wasn't such an easy option. I think that abuse in a marriage and unfaithfulness are both reasons for divorce, but most problems in a marriage can be worked out. Problems that I see in marriage counseling revolve around power and control issues and basic self-centeredness. We want what we want when we want it. In my experience, the major problems in marriage are male-related. It is the guy who is usually unfaithful or abusive or just "falls" out of love.

I also see families that are dysfunctional because there is a problem with alcohol. One of the partners suffers from alcoholism and that creates big problems. Depression is another factor in dysfunctional families. Women who are depressed often have no energy. They have difficulties just getting through the day at work, and come home so exhausted that they cannot function there either. Dads who are depressed seem to be irritable and angry a lot of the time. They have real trouble dealing with their kids, especially their sons.

It makes sense for couples to seek help if drugs, alcohol, depression or whatever is disrupting a marriage. If you are arguing a lot, not communicating, and withdrawing, you need help also. Sometimes men are very reluctant to seek help, but if they don't, they are the big losers. If the marriage breaks up, dads lose their kids.

Kids know that the marriage relationship is important. The biggest fear they have is losing a parent through divorce. Kids want their families to stay together, to work things out. They know how traumatic divorce is. They see it all the time in the families of their friends. Moreover, they know how divorce affects kids. Kids pay a huge price when their parents divorce.

Therefore, work hard on your marriages. It is the most important thing you can do for your kids. Love your spouses, respect them, and be thoughtful of them. Again, the most important relationship in the family is not between parents and kids, but between moms and dads. Take the time needed to make your marriage better.

Reestablish or Remain Connected

Adolescence is a turbulent time for boys. First, they have sexual feelings that they do not understand. Furthermore, they want the freedom to establish their own sense of personhood. Finally, they feel pressure from their peers and also from adults to behave in certain ways. This time can be very confusing for them. How do these young men survive all this turmoil? They survive with help from their families, friends, and mentors – having solid and meaningful relationships.

Adolescents are struggling with identity trying to find out what kind of a person they are becoming. At times, they will push their parents away, wanting more time away from home. But adolescents do not want to cut their ties or separate from their parents completely. What they want is the chance to grow into the individual that they were created to be. Kids come into the world with certain talents and certain personality traits. These develop and blend together to produce an individual. Home, school, parents, teachers, family members, youth leaders and coaches all have an effect on our sons. They help them grow and develop. Hopefully kids grow into sensitive, caring adults who find meaning in their lives and fulfillment in what they do. In a way, parenting is a process of discovery of the gifts that sons were given when they were conceived. Likewise, this discovery includes how to develop those gifts and how to use them to live meaningful lives as adults.

Boys are on a path of discovery; they want parents to help them discover, but they resist being pushed in directions they do not feel are right for them. Sometimes there is a fine line between being pushed and discovering.

Adolescence is a time when our sons need all the help they can get. They need adults who will take the time to connect with them, to love them, and to be there for them. Sons need stable families, where they feel safe. They need limits and boundaries that will protect them and give them a sense of what is right and wrong. Also, they need adults who have their interest at heart and who will spend time and listen to them.

Adolescence is more about growing and testing the waters than about separation. Although kids want separation, they also want the involvement of adults in their lives to help and guide them. Boys have a hidden life, a life that they don't often or readily share with adults. But even in their hidden life, they keep looking over their shoulders to see if there is an adult who cares enough to take the time to find out what's going on.

Joe told me, "My family has always been close. We do a lot of things together. I was brought up to be part of a family. I really enjoy being home on weekends with my mom and dad. We have great times together." That is quite a statement from a 17-year-old boy.

For the adolescent male, having a loving family means he can count on them and their support when the going gets tough. He knows that he always has a place to go and a place where he belongs. This belonging and family connection protects our sons from the harshness of an adolescent world in which they live.

Feldman and Wentzel, from Stanford, demonstrated that the perception boys have of their parents' satisfaction in their marriages affected their sons' social adjustment during adolescence. When parents had satisfactory marriages, kids made good social adjustments. Dr. Bowden of the Cincinnati Children's Hospital found that the children of families who shared an evening meal together did better in school and were less likely to get involved with drugs. The National Longitudinal Study on Adolescent Health found that parent-family connectedness influenced the amount of emotional distress kids felt, how much they used drugs and alcohol, and even to some extent how much they were involved in violent behavior. Other important factors included the presence of parents at home during key periods in the day or whether parents had high or low expectations of their sons' academic performance. The key point, however, was the connection factor. This parameter included the closeness to mom and dad and the sense that they cared for him, loved him, and wanted him.

Role Models

Who do our sons look up to? Who do they pattern their lives after? Who are their role models? We bemoan the fact that there are few role models today. We are well aware of the flaws of movie stars and sport figures. The good news is that most boys find their heroes close to home, i.e., their moms, dads, brothers, sisters, aunts, uncles, and grandparents. Their heroes also include teachers, coaches, and other adults with whom they are involved.

Brent, a 16 year old, told me, "My dad is the person I look up to. I can talk to him about anything. He doesn't get mad; he listens. He showed me how to throw and catch a baseball; he was always at my games. I really count on him."

Sam came from a single-parent home. "It's been tough for my mom. She works hard, but in spite of that, she finds time for me. She helps me with my schoolwork and makes sure I get to practice. Sometimes we go out to supper and a movie on the weekends. She's the greatest."

Steve told me, "Sometimes my dad isn't around. He works a lot out of town. My grandfather would come over or I would go to his house. He showed me how to hit a baseball. We would read together or just hang out. I learned a lot from him. He's a great guy."

These statements tell us how important family role models are. Boys look for and find role models close to home. They look up to and admire these people a lot. What kind of role models are we? How do our kids see us? What does it take to be a good role model? Kids watch us very closely. They want to know what we are really like inside. They watch how we respond to them, if we have time for them and if we listen. Kids can tell if we are really interested in them, or if we are always in a hurry to get somewhere else, or if other things are more important than they are. Moreover, they have learned that we are not perfect – that we blow it occasionally. Down deep, they have a desire for us to be involved with them, not only do they want us, but they need us.

What Parents Can Do To Remain Connected

Take the time to be with your son. Be aware that he connects through activities and through action. Be involved in what he likes to do. Go to his practices and his games. Show him how to hit a baseball, shoot a basketball, etc. Go to his plays. Hang out by getting a hamburger together or by going to a movie. Take him fishing or camping. Find out what he likes to do and do it.

Reorganize your time priorities and make sure he is given time with you when he is young. This routine sets the stage for him to talk to you when he faces the big issues that will confront him during adolescence.

Make sure you tell your son that you love him. Sometimes dads have a hard time telling their sons that they love them. Hugs help also. Get physical. Be sure your son knows how much you appreciate him, and that he is doing a good job. Sons long to hear from their dads that they have done a good job and that they tried hard. Do not expect or demand perfection. It will not happen. Compliment him; don't make him wait for those words.

Be sure to tell him about all the things you treasure about him, what makes him special to you. Notice when he reaches out to be kind to someone and when he shares. Tell him how proud you are of him when he does that.

Try not to ignore tough issues. Sex is a big issue, and so are drugs, depression, and sadness. By ignoring these issues, we give the impression that they are not there, or if we don't bring them up that they will just go away. They won't.

Sex not only can involve pregnancy, but can also involve AIDS and other sexually transmitted diseases. Sex also involves deep emotional feelings. Most boys think they can handle this, but they don't realize what they're getting into or what the consequences are. We have been through a time in our culture when we thought that sexual experience at an early age was all right – that kids could handle it. Now, however, times have changed. There is no such thing as casual sex. The consequences both physically and emotionally are too great. We have learned that kids just can't handle it. They are too young.

Our sons need to know how we feel about these issues. We need to formulate what our standards are and communicate these to him in a way he can understand. The same holds true for drugs. Drugs are available and there is a lot of peer pressure to experiment with them. Be sensitive to whom your sons hang around. They reveal what he is involved with, so know who they are.

By not talking about these things, our sons may make foolish decisions. Letting him know your feelings about these issues may drive him deeper underground, but I feel that ignoring them is riskier. Try to create opportunities for your son to ask questions, and make sure he has the time with you to talk about these things. Bring up the subjects, because he is thinking about them. Addressing them may prevent him from making a bad decision or from getting into a relationship that is potentially dangerous for him.

Values are set by good examples, but they also need clarification. There are limits to behavior that parents must demand from their kids. Kids need structure, something they can count on. Adolescence is often so disorganized that kids find themselves running in all directions at once. They need the organization, the structure of rules and standards to fall back on. When faced at a party with the temptation of drugs or alcohol, because all his buddies are doing them, a young man needs the structure of limits and rules to fall back on. Limits help him and protect him from making bad choices. Do not be fearful of setting limits and demanding conformity to rules – they are, after all, just kids. And kids need limits and direction in their lives.

You can show your son that you understand his situation. While listening, try to put yourself in his shoes. Don't interrupt him with advice. Listen. Then, tell him that you know it's tough being a 17 year old. With the many demands facing teens and with the added demand of peer pressure, adolescence is a challenging time. Often, I have heard dads say, "What's such a big deal about being an adolescent? There are no worries. They are taken care of. All they have to do is go to school and do a few things around the house. Wait until they get into the real world where they will have to be responsible."

They are in a real world, however – an adolescent world. They do have pressures. Life is not easy for them.

Home should be a safe place, a place where your son will be loved, wanted, and respected. Make home a city of refuge that protects your son from the culture and the peer pressure he faces. Create an atmosphere where your son can show his emotions and vulnerabilities openly without feeling shame. Create a place where he can share his ideas, hopes, and dreams without being put down. Make it a place that is fun to be – a place where he feels at home. Parents can make their home that way. As parents, we fail a lot, but we can create this kind of place, a home that is safe and secure, where kids are loved and wanted.

Moreover, home should be a place where his friends are welcome, a safe place that they like to come to also. Get to know his friends. They will tell you a lot about your sons. Find out what they like to do, what movies they go and see, what songs they listen to, and what videos and television programs they watch. Try to develop relationships with your son's friends. Get to know them.

Our kids spend a lot of time at school. What goes on there is important to us, because it is so important to them. Kids need to learn. Keep up with how your son is doing. Most boys will tell their parents that everything is fine at school. Then grades come out and there are C's, D's, and even some F's. Parents are caught by surprise. They should not be. High school is demanding. If you never see your son crack a book at night, common sense tells you he is not doing well. Kids usually need to study at least some time at home. There needs to be study time set aside probably when parents are around and can observe what is going on. The dining room table is a good place to study with the television off. Some kids are highly motivated to study, but most kids are not. Find out about exams, projects, and research papers. It is also a good idea to know your son's teachers, especially if he is having trouble. Keep open the lines of communication to your son and to his teachers. Do not be caught by surprise.

TIPS ON BUILDING A BETTER RELATIONSHIP WITH TEENS
(taken from *The Times-Union*, Jacksonville, Florida, August 30, 1999, written by Patricia Hersch)

BE REAL. The world of regular, everyday adolescents is not what you expect. Get out of denial and get informed. Kids will never accept guidance from adults who are unaware of their reality.

BE AVAILABLE. Most kids think their parents are available to them during the workday for life-threatening emergencies only. But many of the dilemmas of adolescence are less dramatic by adult standards but vitally important to the youngster. Just knowing you're there for them makes a big difference.

BE INVOLVED. No matter what they say, kids like it when their parents show interest in what they are doing. Attend their school and sports activities. Let them choose an activity for the family to do together.

BE THE ADULT YOU ARE. Neither be intimidated nor gullible. You can set boundaries and they will be secretly appreciated. Among those boundaries are curfews, "but this means staying awake until the kids come home."

GET TO KNOW EACH OTHER. Communicate. Eat a meal together. Share your day with them, your feelings, and your past.

NETWORK WITH OTHER PARENTS. The best safeguard of healthy fun for your child is knowing the parents of their friends and communicating with each other.

CREATE WHOLESOME OPTIONS. Create situations for kids to enjoy healthy fun together. Ultimately, the thing adolescents want most is to be with each other. If adults in the community are persistent in setting boundaries and diligent in orchestrating healthy, fun opportunities for kids to socialize, eventually new options can become popular. But involve kids in planning and be patient – it takes a while for something different to catch on.

HUG THEM. Get physical. Tell them you love them and that they are doing a good job.

BE VULNERABLE. Share with them some of your struggles and disappointments.

CREATE SPECIAL TIMES FOR THEM. Do something they like to do.

8

Is Trust a Problem?

How much should we trust our adolescent kids? What do we want to know about them? What do we need to know about them? Is there a difference between prying and concern? Are there areas of a kid's life that are off limits, areas that we shouldn't pry into? These questions are touchy. On the one hand, I am inclined to say, "Sure there are areas of privacy that we as parents should respect, areas into which we should not pry." I think most parents feel that way. Rooms, backpacks, and phone conversations are areas that seem to be off limits for parents. Most kids think so at least. In light of what is happening in the teen subculture, however, I'm not so sure.

In 1998, a report by the National Council on Alcoholism and Drug Dependence showed that 63% of high school seniors reported having been drunk. Kids drive and drink – this is a deadly combination. Almost every year, in every city, driving and drinking end up with wrecks and dead kids. The United States Department of Health and Human Services 1998 survey of high school seniors indicated that 41.4% had used drugs in that school year. Approximately 33% of high school seniors consider themselves smokers. Surveys also show that 56% of girls and 73% of boys have experienced sexual intercourse before age 18, according to the American Academy of Pediatrics. More and more, we are seeing kids getting into real trouble.

Bev Jackson does not hesitate to go through her 18-year-old son's backpack. Nancy Adams sees no problems going into her 11-year-old daughter's bedroom. She does not consider this spying; she calls it concern. "You have to know what is going on all the time. You have to be on top of things."

Her daughter, Megan, has other ideas. "She can go into my room, but she can't snoop. That's not fair. But I'd rather have that go on, than a mom who didn't care."

Cathy, 18, a senior in high school, complained about her mom, "She made me call at 11:30 p.m. on a Friday night and tell her where I was and with whom. I was so embarrassed that I could have died. She also wants to know who my friends are and who I hang out with." Legitimate concern or prying?

Some parents are even hiring agents to follow their kids to see what they are doing. Parents ask agents to find out about their children's friends and where they hang out. Agencies are even getting into Internet chat rooms. Because of anonymity on the Internet, agents can pose as teenagers and find success at having kids tell them what is going on.

Often, the hunches of parents are correct. They find out that their kids are into dangerous things. The world of kids is far more dangerous than it used to be. Driving on a crowded freeway can get out of hand very quickly, even if alcohol is not involved. More and more kids are using drugs and alcohol. Smoking continues to be an issue. Sex is very dangerous with the risk of AIDS and other sexually transmitted diseases, and there is always the risk of pregnancy. Guns are also available to kids. Information on how to build pipe bombs is readily available. The world is different and much more dangerous today than it was for my generation.

Parenting is not for wimps. It is hard. The object of parenting is not being your kid's "buddies." It is protecting them, helping them to grow and develop into productive and caring human beings. When you are involved in their lives, when you know what is going on, you will encounter conflict. Kids don't want their parents to snoop, spy, read their notes, know about their friends, or find out where they hang out. Kids don't like rules, restrictions, and discipline. We know they go underground and live hidden lives. We know they resent us getting into the hidden parts of their lives, but we have to. It is just too dangerous not to. Will this produce more rebellion, more cover-up, and more separation between kids and parents? It could, but this risk must be taken. Parents have to know what is going on.

It is hard to become inquisitive when children are in high school. If you didn't start going into your son's room in grade school or in middle school, then it's going to be harder to do this when he's in high school. But you need to go in and you need to find out what is going on.

Brenda Mixon, an active member of the PTA at her children's schools, said that her kids know that at home, there is an open door policy. "I look through everything: purses, rooms, drawers, and backpacks." Her 16-year old daughter and 14-year-old son have not complained much to this kind of surveillance. Brenda asserts, "If you have always done it, it's not that big of a surprise."

Trust takes time to build up. Kids need to be trusted, but they also need active supervision. Parents need to know what is going on. If you suspect something is going on, you need to find out about it. Parents need to be sensitive to the moods of their children. If a child has withdrawn from his friends and spends a lot of time in his room, then something is going on. If grades have fallen off and a child is angry and irritable, then this is a danger signal. Trouble at school or problems with the law are also signals. Be sensitive to changes in your teenager's personality. This could be a warning signal.

When changes occur, ask your child what's going on, why they don't hang around with their friends anymore. Staying connected and spending time with them gives you the chance to ask questions and receive answers. If you are suspicious of something, follow your instincts.

As I read the Littleton, Colorado, experience and talked to the parents of teenagers, I could not believe parents didn't know what was going on in their homes under their noses – there were pipe bombs being constructed. Are there any areas that are off limits to parents? That depends. If there are any indications that kids are into trouble, or if you suspect things are going on, I would say nothing is off limits.

Do you read notes that are written between your daughter and her boyfriend that you find on her dresser? Sometimes, kids leave things out to inform their parents about things they can't talk about. If my daughter, at the age of 16, were having a serious relationship with a boy, I would want to know what was going on. I would probably read the note. If my daughter told me she was going to spend the night at her friend's house, I would call the friend's mom and talk to her.

Is it important to know who your kid's friends are? Absolutely. Your kids are into the same things that their friends are into. In the adolescent subculture, friends think and behave the same way. Conformity is the "in" thing. Don't think for a second that your kids don't do what their friends do. They often say they don't, but they do. This is the standard argument that parents hear from their teenagers, but in most cases, it just is not true – your kids behave the way their friends do. It is good to know your children's friends and it's good to know their parents. Also, it is important to communicate with their parents. When a 16 year old tells you that she is staying overnight at a friend's house, or that John's mom is letting him go to an unsupervised party, check it out. Don't take everything at face value.

How far should trust go? Is everything suspect? These questions are tough. Trust is mutual. Being connected to our children, spending time with them, listening, helps them trust us. Kids may not like what we are doing, but if we have established this trust base over the years, they will realize that we have a vital interest in them and what they are doing. Many of the kids that I deal with are glad that their parents take an interest in them and are concerned about them.

All too often, parents are reluctant about talking to their children about topics like sex, drugs, alcohol, and smoking. Your children need to know how you feel about these subjects. Start early when kids are young. Be willing to talk and to listen. By talking about the difficult subjects, you communicate how you feel about things and what the rules are. These rules must be laid down, and the consequences for breaking them need to be set, so that there are no misunderstandings. Behavior has consequences. Kids need to learn this lesson early in life. Teach them.

One of the difficult parts of parenting is protection. We can't protect our kids if we don't know what they are into. Whatever it takes, find out what your kids are into. The stakes are just too high not to know. Kids don't realize what a dangerous, violent world they live in. Kids have poor judgment. They have to learn. Teach them, but, while you are teaching them, protect them.

9

Troubled Kids

Obviously, very troubled kids attend our schools. Schools are a place where kids learn. What happens if your kid, for some reason, has difficulty learning? As 5 year olds, kids are excited about school. They can't wait to get there. They want to learn. But, for some reason, when they do get there, learning is just harder than they thought it would be. Most of the rewards given out in the classroom are for work well done, e.g., spelling words correctly, completing the math problems, and pronouncing words correctly. All kids don't have this aptitude. Some kids just don't do very well in school. Classmates pick this fact up very early. They know who the smart kids are and who the "dumb" kids are. Very early there is a division of kids into fast learner and slow learner groups. How does it feel to be branded a slow learner?

Some kids have trouble focusing in on tasks. They are so hyperactive that they cannot sit still. Their thoughts are so scattered that they can't narrow them down on spelling words or addition problems. I see kids like this in my practice. They are not dumb kids; they just can't focus in on their work or sit still long enough to get it done.

John, 7, was like that. He was in second grade. His first grade teacher had told his mom that he could not focus in on his work nor sit still. He was up, out of his seat, constantly walking around the room talking to his friends. John was tested and found to have ADHD (attention deficit hyperactivity disorder). John responded to medication and this situation was turned around. I have seen lots of kids like John. Often medication helps them, as it did with John. Structured study habits also help. John's mom went over his math problems with him, called out his spelling words, and listened to him read. This routine went on every night after supper, sometimes for two hours, whatever it took. John's dad was also involved in his studies.

It was important for John that this situation was picked up early. It is easy for a first grader to get discouraged about learning, struggle, and then just give up. John, who was actually a bright kid, would have been labeled a slow learner by his classmates at a time when being labeled like that was so harmful. John would have been so ashamed that he couldn't do the work.

Some professionals believe that ADHD does not exist. Others believe that it is diagnosed too often. Yet others feel that medication is used too frequently. I do not agree with these points. I feel that ADHD does exist, that it runs in families, and that medications can help. So does structured study time and counseling. I have seen many kids who have ADHD respond to medications. For some, medication literally turned their lives around. They are transformed from kids who could not focus or get their schoolwork done to kids who could get their work done and could focus. If these symptoms turn up, it is important that parents take their sons to a professional, a psychiatrist or a psychologist, for help.

Other kids suffer from dyslexia. They have special problems with math or reading and get branded as slow learners also. They struggle; learning is difficult for them. There is an interesting correlation between reading and getting involved with the criminal justice system. In Florida, if a boy cannot read by the time he is through the third grade, he has a 90% chance of being involved with the criminal justice system. In Florida, it costs $37,000 a year to incarcerate someone, more than it costs to send him to Harvard. You would think that it would be cost-effective to work with these kids so they can read.

Trouble starts early in school. Some kids do have problems learning, and early detection is of great importance. Teachers, nowadays, look for kids who have problems learning. Parents need to know their children's teachers and find out what their concerns are. Together they can address a child's learning problems.

In our culture, reading, spelling, and math are keys to jobs as an adult. In Jacksonville, Florida, high school graduates who attend the junior college often have to take remedial classes in math, English, and social science. In fact, 80% of them do. The problems of learning are complex, but often we can pick out students who have problems learning early. Many of these kids can be helped.

We also fail to detect depression in kids. We lose 5,000 kids a year due to suicide. Most of these kids are depressed. For every one who is successful at suicide, more than 200 attempt it and fail. This adds up to a lot of kids who are depressed. Even more astounding, 1 adolescent in 4, i.e., 25% of the adolescent population, considers suicide. Depression in kids is present all around us, even in our homes.

Depression is often missed in adolescence, although the signs are recognizable. Anger is something I see a lot of in depressed kids. They seem to be mad and irritable most of the time. Everything is an argument. Boys become very defiant and oppositional. They may also look and sound depressed. Often they retreat to their rooms, isolating themselves from their friends. Grades can drop; they get in trouble in school. Personality changes go on right before your eyes. Kids who were outgoing, friendly, and happy turn into angry, withdrawn, sullen kids. They may also be preoccupied with death and dying. Some of these kids talk about suicide.

Kids also show the classical signs of depression. They look and feel sad and depressed – they cry often. Also, they have no energy and are unmotivated. Often, they have problems sleeping. At times, they lose their appetite and lose weight.

Jim was a typical 16 year old. He liked to hang out with his friends, go to the mall, and watch television. All through school, his grades were good. He had to work for grades, but he was willing to do that most of the time. He started out his sophomore year in good shape, but, after a few weeks, his mom noticed that Jim spent more time by himself. Instead of hanging out with his friends, he went to his room and shut the door. His grades dropped, and he was in trouble in geometry and chemistry. These school problems were unusual for Jim. His mom noticed the changes that were going on and became concerned. Jim told her that he did not feel good, that he felt like crying, and that he was sad a lot. He also told her that he had trouble sleeping at night and that he was not motivated to study.

I put Jim on an antidepressant, and, in several weeks, he was back to his old self again. Jim's mom picked up the fact that he was depressed and got him into treatment. Depression can be treated, but it needs to be diagnosed first. Try to find out what is going on with your son. Ask him how he feels and why he is withdrawing. Let him know that you are concerned.

Bill, 16, was in my office, somewhat reluctantly, with his mom. You would have noticed him anywhere. His hair was long in the back and shaved on the sides. He had a silver earring in his left ear. His pants were baggy, and he was dressed in black. His eyes were downcast – he appeared sullen and angry. His mom and his teachers were concerned. As a smart kid, his elementary and middle school years had gone well. Then things started to change in the ninth grade. His grades dropped from A's and B's to C's and occasional D's. Everything was an argument, as Bill became more oppositional, defiant, and angry. He began to retreat to his room more and stopped hanging out with his old friends. Most of the time he spent listening to his tapes alone in his room. This outgoing child had turned inward. His whole personality changed.

Jim was 17, in his last year of high school. He had been a good student until six months ago. Then he noticed that he was starting to become sad. Tears were always close to the surface. Moreover, Jim had trouble sleeping, often waking up and not being able to go back to sleep. Finally, he would wake up at 4 a.m. and lie there awake until time to get up for school. He felt tired all the time and dragged around without any energy. Because he was so tired, it was hard for him to study. He also didn't feel much like eating and lost some weight. Jim did not feel like hanging around with his friends either. His grades started to fall and that really concerned him. As he relayed his misery, with tears in his eyes, he told me that he even felt like taking his own life.

Both these young men had one thing in common – they were clinically depressed. Jim showed the classic signs of depression. He had problems sleeping and eating. His energy was down, and his grades fell because he did not have the energy to study. Although he was tired all the time, his most alarming sign was suicidal thoughts. I always ask my depressed patients if they are suicidal or not. This information can save lives.

Bill was depressed also, but his depression presented itself with anger, sullenness and confrontational behavior. It also showed up in rather profound personality changes. He went from being an outgoing, happy kid who got good grades to someone who was angry, defiant, and confrontational. He also looked different and hung around with either a new crowd or retreated to his room.

These kids were depressed. Their parents were concerned enough to bring them to see me, which is often difficult for parents to do. Parents tend to fail to recognize depression in their children, often thinking that it is another stage they are going through or that they will get over it. Parental denial can play a part in missing the signs of depression. "This can't be happening to my child. What does he or she have to be depressed about?"

Depression tends to run in families. I found out that Bill and Jim came from families that had depression in them somewhere. Bill had an aunt who was depressed and Jim's uncle had a problem with alcoholism. Depression has a large genetic component. This genetic component manifests itself in brain chemistry. Parents need to be sensitive to the signs of depression in young people. Depression in adolescents does not always resemble depression in adults. It shows up in other ways.

SIGNS THAT POINT TO DEPRESSION

1. anger, irritability, sullenness, defiance, oppositional behavior, anger outbursts
2. withdrawal from friends, spends a lot of time alone in his room
3. impulsiveness, unpredictability, emotional, worried, tense
4. lethargic, lacks energy, sluggish, less outgoing
5. problems sleeping, waking up at night, sleeping more than usual
6. loss of appetite, weight loss, no interest in food
7. problems concentrating and getting into schoolwork
8. grades dropping
9. problems at school, skipping classes, not turning in work, in detention

10. acting out, getting drunk, acting out sexually, taking drugs
11. taking more risks, driving fast
12. pervasive sadness, depression, crying
13. preoccupation with death, dying, suicide
14. hard on himself, feels that he is a failure, feels that nothing is going right
15. low self-esteem

All these symptoms won't show up at the same time in a depressed boy. Often, these kids are angry. They also usually undergo a dramatic personality change, from outgoing to withdrawn. Furthermore, they become less involved with sports, their grades drop, and they lose interest in things with which they were once involved. Sometimes there is also a dramatic change in how they dress, how they wear their hair, and with whom they hang out.

Depression is a biochemical illness having to do with brain cells – how neurons communicate with one another. To treat major depression, you have to change brain chemistry. I use antidepressants for this purpose. Jim responded to antidepressants and is doing well in college. Bill would never try medication. He never came back for follow up. Depressed kids aren't the only angry kids, but when I see a lot of anger, I think of depression first.

When I was the team physician at Gainesville High School, I used to walk across the street at lunchtime to the high school and eat lunch with kids whom I knew. Often, I'd stop by the group of kids eating together on the lawn. They called themselves the "out" group. They considered themselves not part of the "in" group. Who made up the "in" groups? The athletes, the cheerleaders, the good-looking, popular kids, those who had money, cars and those in Student Government. And the others? They were just outsiders. You could tell which group a kid belonged to just by seeing with whom he hung out.

Can you imagine what it feels like to be excluded? I remember not being invited to a hayride when I was an 8th grader. That was so painful. I still remember it after all these years. Even worse, can you imagine being tormented, shoved against lockers, and threatened every day? Yet, some students face this humiliation often.

Troubled and angry kids go to our schools. Some of them are our children. If one is sensitive to what is going on, it is not that difficult to pick up who the angry, isolated, picked-on kids are at the local high school. Often, they stand out. For example, some dress differently, usually in black. Their hairstyles are also different, with black and silver the dominant colors. Frequently, these kids hang out together.

Angry kids are in our schools – kids angry enough to kill. I am certain that we can spot the troubled kids. Their problems do not start in the 11th or 12th grades. The signs are there early on. These include trouble with reading, math, and spelling, trouble sitting at a desk, and trouble getting schoolwork done. Kids who are excluded, who cannot make their Little League teams, and who are not invited to the parties become angry. Also, kids who are not part of the "in" crowd feel excluded, i.e., those who are not cute, not smart, not popular, and not athletic. How would it feel to wake up one day and realize that you were not accepted? For a lot of kids, more than we want to admit, school is not the friendly place that it ought to be. For many of these kids, it is hard to go to school, let alone do their work.

Being part of something, just belonging, is so important for kids. Just being recognized for something, such as sports, dancing, or studies, is so significant. One time a sophomore boy told me, "No one will ever remember me here at high school. I never played football. I never got good grades, and I never was elected to anything. The only thing I'll be remembered for is being bad, and I'll be better at being bad than anyone in this school." And he was!

If you ask 50 kids who the "dangerous" kids are at their high school, the same kids make almost all the lists. Kids know, so how come teachers don't?

The good news is that we can treat depression and ADHD. Kids can learn to read and can be helped. We need to be alert and spot troubled kids early. This way, we can get them the help they need.

10
Violence in Us

A few years ago, at a Methodist conference center, a group of us got away together for a weeklong retreat. Some of these people were friends whom I knew because of shared interests. This retreat had great potential. On Wednesday of that week, the group divided into teams. One team was given, for no apparent reason, all the advantages for success in a game. On the other hand, my team could not accomplish its goal, no matter how hard we tried. We just did not have the resources. How frustrated I felt! I remember getting into someone's face and yelling – I was so angry. The feeling of being powerless was so adverse.

What caught me by surprise was how angry I had become, and how close this anger was to the surface of my conscious self. I felt it with an intensity that I never knew existed.

Before this experience, I had not seen myself as an angry, violent person. When I was a kid, I had not gotten into a lot of fights. And I don't remember feeling this kind of rage welling up in me. I was ready to fight, to knock someone's head off over some stupid game in which I was treated unfairly. Although I knew that I had been set up and that the game would be over, the rage was present. It just intensified.

Amazed by my reaction, I did not want to admit that I had that much anger in me. It was right there, right beneath the surface. With a little provocation, I just exploded. Since then, I have been more aware of my anger. I get glimpses of it when, driving into work, I am cut off by some car, or when I am caught in a situation where I feel powerless or vulnerable. At times, when I get into heated discussions, I feel angry, intense. Anger is in me, and it is close to the surface. It's amazing how easy it is to activate this anger.

In 1978, Paul Tournier, a Swiss physician and counselor, wrote a book called *The Violence Within* that talks about the violence and anger that is within us all. I agree with much of what he had to say because of my own anger and because of the anger I see in my patients.

Dr. Tournier makes the point that society tolerates anger and violence. We're all upset about the violence in a high school in Littleton, Colorado, and rightly so. But violence goes on every weekend in Jacksonville, Florida, where I live. Just spend time in the emergency room at University Hospital, and you will see patients with gunshot wounds, stabbings, and beatings, all kinds of violence. Although we have tolerated inner city violence for a long time, now we see it differently – it's in a suburban high school, close to home.

Dr. Tournier goes on to say, "All conflicts have broadly the same pattern. There is always a privileged party, standing by an established order, which benefits its members, the reigning party in power. These privileged people do not need to have recourse to make violence, because they have the law and power on their side." In our culture, here I am, white, male, physician, power-ful, yet, still feeling the anger in me, right below the surface. What do the less powerful do with their anger? How about the kids who are shoved against lockers and taunted on a regular basis at the schools they attend? What about their anger? How do they react to it? We know how some of them react all too well.

How do we handle our aggression, our anger? I'll tell you how I handle mine. I rationalize that my anger is legitimate, while another person's anger is to be condemned. My anger is for a cause – someone has been violated, hurt or treated badly. My anger is righteous indignation; my anger is justifiable. So, I rationalize and deny. The problem with this justification is that my kids and grandkids pick it up. They see it in my racist atti-tudes, my sexist attitudes, and my prejudices. They see my an-ger, my attitudes, and they often adopt them. Kids learn to hate at home – we teach them. We are more capable of hate, anger, and violence than we think.

Our media is accused of being too violent. I agree that it has gone much too far. I can't believe the violence that video games expose my 10 year-old grandson to. They are so graphic. Do you think that they would be tolerated for one minute if we as a culture were not fascinated with violence, or that we as human beings were not violent ourselves?

Given the right situation, I could explode with anger and violence. I usually hide this from myself. I deny it, but it's there. How I deal with my anger and the violence to which it leads is very important. Society puts limits on what I can do, and rightly so.

Just after World War II, Dr. Carl Menninger, the well-known psychiatrist, visited Buchenwald with a group of American physicians. Buchenwald was a Nazi concentration camp in which more than 100,000 people from German-occupied countries were killed. Dr. Menninger remarked, "My colleagues were horrified at what they saw. They could not believe their eyes and found it hard to accept that human beings were capable of such horrors. I was horrified, but not surprised."

Why did Dr. Menninger react the way he did? He knew what human beings are like, what they are capable of. He stated, "Man is in fact violent." We think, often, that this violence is an anomaly, an exceptional deviation, confined to a few sick persons. This is reassuring, but it may not be true. There is violence in all of us. We are all capable of it under the right circumstances.

Today, young males carry out most of the violence in our society against young males. When a boy's anger escalates unchecked, it may erupt as violence – violence against other young males, violence against himself, violence against society.

Most of us think that violence happens in other families, to other people's kids, i.e., inner city kids, gang members, serial killers, rapists, but does not involve our sons or the children of families we know. If we talk to family members, however, we find that an uncle committed suicide, a son was beaten up at college, a husband was physically abusing his wife, or someone in the family was murdered. We live in a violent world. Our sons are vulnerable to violence. They see extreme violence of one kind or another – in school, on the street, on television, in the movies, on video games and, sadly, even at home. Almost all of us are touched by violence. Violence is in our own families and families in our neighborhoods.

When boys are young, they roughhouse with males, usually their dads. Sometimes this rowdiness can get rough. At times, it is hard for a young boy to know the difference between roughhousing and violence. Sometimes a dad has to say, "I think this is getting too rough, that hurt." Boys need to learn to separate roughhousing, action that they love, from violence. When is roughhousing too rough? When does teasing become bullying? When does boldness become dangerous risk taking? We need to teach our sons how to handle and deal with anger and violence before situations go too far.

But why are so many boys and young men violent? Dr. Pollack feels that disconnection at an early age is the cause. It is the end result of being pushed into an adult world before boys are ready, without the support and love they need. Males become seriously disconnected, and then go behind a mask and express the only acceptable male emotion – anger. When anger grows unchecked, it can erupt into violence. This violence is directed inward, at himself, and outward toward others or even at society. Dr. Pollack claims that violence is the last link in the chain that starts with disconnection.

Violence is also about shame and honor. Failing to know how to fight or not wanting to fight may be considered disgraceful, not "manly." To protect his honor and prevent shame, a boy may strike out against younger or weaker boys. Violence often goes a long way in protecting a boy from shame. I can still feel the shame from refusing to fight when I was 14. This goes back to the boy code concepts of being tough, independent, and manly.

Violence is deeply embedded in our society. It's not only in the inner city or in the woods of Michigan or Montana. It's also found at an unguarded moment in religious people who are at a retreat. It's on highways when reckless drivers cut other cars off. Violence is all around and, if we look deeply enough, inside us also.

Handling Anger

Frank was an average 8th grader. He was not that big, not that athletic. He did, however, have some buddies with whom he hung out. They went to the mall and played video games. Mike had a locker next to Frank's. When they showed up at their lockers at the same time, Mike would shove his locker door across Frank's locker so that Frank had to wait until Mike was finished before he could get into his locker. This had gone on since September. Frank was somewhat intimidated by Mike. He was fearful that Mike would beat him up if he did anything about the locker problem. One day, however, Frank reached his boiling point. After Mike's locker door slammed across his locker, Frank grabbed Mike by the shoulders and slammed his back against the locker.

"Don't ever do that again," Frank told Mike angrily. Mike was taken off guard by this action, but he backed off.

How does one handle bullies? This is a problem for kids, parents, teachers, everyone involved in schools. It is one thing to shove a bully against a locker, but what if you are so intimidated that you couldn't possibly do that? How do you control your anger at being bullied?

We know that excessive teasing and bullying can be very problematic for kids. They feel helpless and powerless. They feel humiliated, angry. A whining, complaining kid often becomes a kid who is hard to relate to. The kid who is picked on feels isolated and alone at the very time that he needs help and support. If he can find a gun, he feels powerful all of a sudden. And he is. As an example, Eric Harris and Dylan Klebold, the Columbine High School students who shot up their school, were picked on and taunted by their classmates, especially by the athletes. Their sense of powerlessness may have played a part in the shootings. Certainly these were angry kids.

All of us have been in situations where we felt powerless. Most of the time, these situations did not last very long. I can usually control the anger that I feel on the expressway. However, I don't know how I would react if I were a high school kid and I was teased and intimidated every day at school. And what if I had access to guns? Gun access really changes the equation. It enables the powerless to become very powerful. Most kids do not resort to this type of violence. I feel, however, that all of us are capable of anger that can escalate into rage, which can turn into violence – the type of violence that we read about or see on television every day. When you combine depression and family pathology with disconnection from adults, intimidation at school, drugs and alcohol, then you have potential for violence. When I read about kids being shot at school, I am saddened, but not all that surprised.

How do we handle anger? Where do boys learn how to handle anger? Where do they learn what is acceptable? They learn from us, parents, especially dads. They watch us closely. All of us get angry. How do we react? We are role models for anger control.

Suppose I am riding in a car with my grandson and a guy cuts me off. I get mad. I wish at that moment that I had a tank. I jam my foot on the gas. Wait a minute – what am I doing? What is going on? For one thing, I have the eyes of an 11-year-old grandson on me. He knows that I am upset, and he watches to see what I will do and how I will react.

As men, fathers, grandfathers, we must be role models for anger control for our sons and grandsons. We must be in control of our anger. Kids watch how we react. All of us become angry from time to time. That is just how life is. But we can't allow our anger to get out of control, go unchecked, and go into rage. When this happens, all of us have the potential of becoming violent. Can we control our anger as adult males? I think so.

Ken and Patty were in my office. They were having problems with their marriage. It all came to a head three nights ago when Ken came home at 8:30 p.m. after working late. "He was so angry that he slammed the door, yelled something at me and jammed his fist right through the wall. His hand was bruised and bleeding. I was terrified; I have never seen Ken react that way. We have had arguments before, but never like this. For the first time, I was really frightened."

Ken told me that work was getting very stressful. He was working a lot of hours, and was just fed up with everything. "I just lost control," he told me. I asked him if his boss made him mad, would he "lose control" with him? He got the point. Most of us can control our anger. We don't usually lose control in situations where this behavior will get us into trouble. We can control ourselves. We do it all the time.

Even at a more basic level, how do we react to groups that we are not part of? If you accept the idea that anger can grow out of intolerance, and that, when anger explodes, it can cause violence, then we need to look at our intolerance level. How do we react to groups of people who are different than we are?

Racial hatred is not born in a schoolroom, on a playground, or in the streets, but in a home, my home. My kids pick up my attitude. This year, two young men killed a young gay man in Wyoming. We were all horrified by the brutality of this murder. Where do you think these young men first learned about this type of intolerance? I bet somewhere in this story is an adult male family member who expressed intolerance to gays, and this attitude was picked up. These two young men acted out of intolerance and hate. In our culture, which is very pluralistic, there are many things that we do not agree with. These things range from lifestyle, cultural background, drugs, religious or non-religious ways of thinking, political philosophies, etc. How important it is for us to be tolerant of people even though we differ on how we think or live out our lives. Our kids pick up our attitudes. What are we showing them? Are we teaching them tolerance and respect or intolerance and hatred?

People who are taught to care about others, who are taught tolerance, and who feel connected to male role models are the ones who rarely, if ever, let their anger get out of control to the extent that they commit acts of violence. If a young man feels cared for and remains connected to his family, then he is more likely to care for others and feel a connection to other people.

I have a grandson, Hunter, who lives on the other side of town. I have to make the effort to be involved in his life. The other night, I was at his ballgame. There were lots of parents there also. I watched one dad talk on his cell phone the entire game. He was there in person, but he was not there emotionally. He was out of contact with his son. We need to be there in person and in contact emotionally. Kids sense whether we're there or not – they know. Staying in contact and connected can bring rich dividends. It really impacts a life and lays the foundation for a great relationship for our whole lives. What could we possibly do that would be more meaningful for us as dads?

Our sons are watching us. They are picking up how frequently we say one thing and do another. They see us when we are angry and how we react. They are very sensitive to this. So, what type of modeling behavior can we be involved in that will teach our sons to be empathetic, tolerant, and thoughtful of others?

How can we, as males, create an atmosphere, a place, and a time when our sons will share what is going on in their lives and how they are really feeling? Certainly, it starts with staying connected, by giving them the time together that provides the opportunity for sharing and getting into their feelings. They usually won't do this around the dinner table, where a big sister or little brother is listening. It won't be in a car full of his friends riding home from a movie. It could happen while you are tucking him into bed or when just the two of you are eating hamburgers at Burger King. It may be after you share with him your disappointment over not getting a promotion. At times, it is the sharing of your own disappointments, your own imperfections that opens the door for him to share his feelings. Sharing comes often at least expected times. Create the atmosphere. Provide the time and listen with empathy. It takes real courage sometimes for sons to tell us that friends have let them down or that they are being bullied at school. It is hard for boys to talk about being humiliated, picked on, and shamed at school. It is hard for them to talk about feeling "left out" of something, how it feels not to be invited to a party.

I think that we need to raise boys differently. Our sons need to be taught how to be sensitive to their feelings. When they are hurt, shamed, or left out, they need to be taught how to deal with these adversities. All boys have very similar feelings, however, most of them do not act out on these feelings as did Eric Harris or Dylan Klebold. Being connected to a caring, supportive family helps dealing with feelings of powerlessness.

Obviously, this connection has to go further than just talking. Many young men feel "spiritually empty," according to Dr. James Garbarino of Cornell. "We must teach boys how to deal with problems other than through rage," he states. Kids who have spiritual foundations seem to have an empathetic understanding of others, that is, how to put themselves in the other person's situation. Boys who are allowed to deal with their own feelings are sensitive to others. We need to raise boys who are allowed to be sensitive to their own feelings, so that they can be sensitive to others.

There is anger deep inside all of us. We have all felt it from time to time. It is there. Our sons and grandsons feel it also. It is imperative that we teach them how to handle and control that anger and how to prevent that anger from erupting into the rage that explodes into violence.

11

Violence in the Culture

Time magazine carried an interesting article by Nancy Gibbs in its May 17, 1999, issue. Its title was "Noon in the Garden of Good and Evil."

Ms. Gibbs begins by making the point that long ago we decided, as a nation, to keep church and state separate. But Columbine brought to our attention changes that involve both church and state. She makes the point that the lines between the sacred and secular are blurred. Ministers call on lawmakers to pass gun control laws, while lawmakers call for religious revival. The events in Littleton, Colorado, send out a "spiritual signal," the chance to ask questions that relate not to church or state, but to both.

Ms. Gibbs continues, "The Columbine tragedy didn't start out as a front-page story about the battle between good and evil. But it has been moving there, as the trauma overflowed the argument about guns and culture and spilled into other realms. With each passing day of shock and grief, you could almost hear the church bells tolling in the background, calling the country into a different debate – one that does not look for reasons but for meaning."

At first, the questions were about Harris and Klebold, questions that we could not avoid and to which we did not have the answers. The talk shows blamed the culture, guns, parents, movies, video games. These explanations, however, leave too much unresolved for those who think the tragedy has to do with inherent evil, that which is hidden and that which is not so hidden in all of us. Perhaps the boys were not actually evil, but a product of evil, the dark force we meet in Star Wars. We

95

do not like to think about or worry about the forces of evil, but they are there. The reality of that has to be present after what has happened.

Cassie Bernall was the young lady who was asked if she believed in God, and then was gunned down when she replied, "Yes." Both evil and good now had faces. The martyrs that we know about are from past ages. They did not carry backpacks or think about prom dresses. Cassie's story included transformation. She was once lost to bad friends, drugs, even witchcraft. Then she went to a camp, a Christian camp, the previous summer. She was transformed there, rescued. She became involved with inner city kids, went to a Bible study, dropped her old friends, the drugs, and the witchcraft. She even wore a What Would Jesus Do bracelet.

Cassie's Christian friends are now being asked new questions – questions about faith. Kids who want to talk are flooding youth ministries. 150 Columbine kids showed up at their Young Life leader's house in Littleton after the tragedy. At a Denver prayer lunch recently, faith and practice sat down together. Everyone attending was asked by organizer Don Reverts to agree to mentor an "at risk" kid to "change the city."

Maybe it is time that we ask questions. Is there evil in us, in our personalities, at the deepest part of our beings? Is there an evil force, one that surrounds us, permeates us, influences us? Maybe we have heard too often and for so long how good we are and that we are getting better. Are we really all that good? Carl Rogers likened humans to onions. When you peel off the outer layers, you reach a core of goodness. Maybe, just maybe, if we peeled off the outer layers of our personalities, we would reach an inner core of badness. Maybe we are more like Cassie Bernall than we think. Maybe we need transformation and conversion, not only ourselves, but our culture also.

These questions are not being discussed by talk show hosts or by news analysts, but they are being talked about everywhere high school kids gather with youth ministers, with families around dinner tables, and with friends over coffee. We all agree that something has to happen, something has to change – maybe it's conversion, transformation, radical change. Littleton gives us a chance to do just that.

A good look at our culture tells us a lot about ourselves, about you and me. 50% of all marriages end in divorce. You can't turn on television without seeing people violently killed. Vivid sex is so common that it's expected. Video games desensitize 8 year olds to guns, blood, and killing. No matter where we go, we encounter violence.

According to *Crime in the United States*, the 1997 crime report put out by the United States Department of Justice:

- Someone is murdered every 29 minutes in our country.
- A violent crime is committed every 19 seconds.
- Aggravated assault occurs every 31 seconds.
- In 1997, 442 young men and 126 young women, aged 13-16, were murdered. (240 were white; 289 were black.)
- 1,374 males, aged 17-19, were murdered in 1997. During the same time, 1,205 females were murdered. Guns were used most of the time – 477 times involving kids aged 13-16 and 1,325 times involving kids aged 17-19.

Thus, more than 3,000 teens a year are murdered. This adds up to 240 Columbines a year.

The violence that permeates our culture increasingly involves adolescent males. Boys and young men are at risk for all kinds of violence: from car accidents to fighting. Violent crime, murder, suicide, accidents, and injuries cause more serious problems for kids than infections, heart disease, lung problems, etc. Some examples:

- 78% of all unintentional deaths of kids are caused by car accidents. (75% are males)
- 33% of all violent crimes are involved with males aged 12 to 19.
- Murder is the 2nd leading cause of death during adolescence. (males are 400% more likely to be murdered than females)
- From 1979-1991, 40,000 kids aged 14-19 died from gunshot wounds.
- The firearm death rate among male teens (15-19) doubled from 1985-1994.
- Suicide is the 3rd leading cause of death for those aged 15-24. Young male suicides are 4 times as common as young female suicides.

From these statistics, we can see that boys are at high risk for violence in a culture that tolerates violence.

If you have kids or grandkids, you know about the media, how violent it is. An inexhaustible amount of violence invades our living rooms, our homes, our lives, and we have little or no control over it. Cable television is present in most homes now, which just expands the choices. One can't flip the channels without running into a violent movie, a violent television drama, or a violent news story. Even the cartoons are violent. Television commercials, although not particularly violent, portray young men as young, cool, and aloof. They often are involved in risk-taking behavior, e.g., fast driving, sky diving, bungee-jumping. This behavior reinforces the traditional male stereotype of being cool, tough, and macho.

When I was a kid, and things got out of control at school, kids would challenge each other to a fight. I remember two really big, strong kids getting into an argument and going out back of our high school to settle it. These kids were very capable of hurting each other with their fists. On the way out of school, reason prevailed, things calmed down, and they walked away.

In contrast, today, young men are more apt to strike out and become violent. Why? First, we were not exposed to the violence on television as kids are today. Exposure begins at age 2 or 3, years before a child can tell the difference between reality and fantasy. This exposure continues two to three hours a day, all the way through adolescence. What does television teach our kids? Even good guys use killing as a first resort. Violence is a normal reaction. Heroes use violence to solve problems. If a hero does not like what a person does, he just blows him away. Another contributing factor is the availability of guns. Now, two hotheaded kids can just decide to shoot it out. Fistfights were bad enough, but now we fight with deadly weapons. Where once we backed down from fighting, especially if we knew we would lose, now, with guns, this fear is taken away. Guns make everyone equal. A small, physically weak kid can win this confrontation with deadly consequences.

Does television influence our kids? A lot of advertisers think so. They spend millions trying to influence our children. Preschool kids watch two to three hours of television a day. By the time kids are 8, they watch four hours a day.

Parents rarely control what kids see on television. In fact, many parents use television as a babysitter to keep kids quiet and in another room. If the home has 2 sets, parents and kids do not watch television together. Moreover, they do not talk about what television exposes them to. This reticence prevents parents from helping their kids understand and interpret what they see.

For a long time, critics have been saying that the 20 or 30 hours a week of television not only damages kids, but also undermines our society. Violence is not the only concern. When kids watch television, they can't play baseball, have fun with friends, or do their homework. They are not reading either. One Canadian study showed that when multi-channel television arrived in a remote mountain town in the 1970s, reading comprehension went down. For years, we have heard from television executives that violence on television does not teach kids to act violently. Psychologists and other experts disagree. They contend that there is a connection between television violence and violent behavior. Two Surgeon Generals have supported the idea that television violence promotes violence. So have The American Medical Association, The American Pediatric Association, the American Academy of Child Psychiatry, and the American Psychological Association! They have determined that television violence does influence behavior in our kids. Kids learn from television: what clothes to buy, what cereal to eat, what toys to play with, and, yes, how to react in explosive ways. Our perceptiveness confirms this. Nothing is shocking anymore. Kids have seen it all on television. Perhaps the morbid fascination that so many kids have with death is that it is the final experience, the only experience that they have not experienced personally. One can't experience it without actually going through it. We lose 5,000 kids a year to suicide.

If our kids are into video games, then we think that at least they are safe from the violence seen on television. Wrong! I just spent some time looking at video games. My 11-year-old grandson has one called Resident Evil 2, which follows Resident Evil 1. This game contains scene after scene of violence, with blood all over the place. A young woman runs through the streets until she finds a gun shop. When she bursts inside, she comes face to face with the gun shop owner who points a shotgun at her. She yells, "Don't shoot; I'm human." This saved her. Soon, zombies break into the store and are shot by the owner. The head of one of the zombies is kicked off his body. Another zombie groans and he gets shot again. The young lady then runs out of the store with a gun and ammunition and runs through the town. More zombies attack her. Four more are shot, all of them covered with blood. This same scene repeats itself. Later on, zombies are seen eating a dead body. All of this happened in the first ten minutes of the game. My grandson told me that Resident Evil 2 was so scary that he did not play it at night and that Resident Evil 3 was even scary during the day. I understood.

Time/CNN Teen Poll

The following results are from a telephone poll of
329 teenagers who play video games.
Sampling error is ± 5.4%.

How many hours do you spend each week playing video games?
None	13%
1 to 4	70%
5 to 9	12%
10 or more	4%

Have you ever played games like Doom, Quake, Duke Nukem or Redneck Rampage, and if so, how often?
Yes, play regularly	10%
Yes, played a few times	50%
No, never played	40%

Do your parents have rules about playing video games, and do you follow them?
Yes, and always follow	24%
Yes, but don't always follow	18%
No, parents don't have rules	58%

Later, I looked at some of my grandson's magazines that advertise these games. One was named *Official U.S. Playstation*

Magazine. One company, Activision, was presenting "Tai Fu – Wrath of the Tiger."

Start your bad self through 20 intense levels of sweeping rivers and dense bamboo forests on your quest to defeat the dragon master. Take on lethal animal enemies inspired by Chinese legend, including muscle-bound snakes and ferocious wild boar.

Tai Fu, they told the potential buyer was Chinese for "kick ass."

Another ad shows a dark figure with a raised 45, with the words "Deploy – Destroy – then relax over a cold one." A skeleton is depicted across the page. Another caption read "Dead in the Water/Live Fast – Die Wet."

I will destroy you in the battle mode.

I will destroy you in the two-player split screen mode.

I will destroy you in the combat cable link mode.

I will destroy you, maggot.

This type of information continues, page after page. These are the catalogs our kids and grandkids are looking at.

Yet another example is *Basketball Diary*, a movie about a high school male who dreamed that he went into his high school with a gun and blew students away.

The Internet tells kids how to make pipe bombs and where they can buy guns. All this information is readily available to kids.

Time/CNN Teen Poll

The following results are from a telephone poll of 409 American teenagers 13 to 17 years old taken to TIME/CNN on April 27-29, 1999, by Yankelovich Partners, Inc. Sampling error is ± 4.8%. "Not sures" omitted.

Do you use the Internet for things like e-mail, chat rooms or visiting websites?

Yes   82%

Have you ever seen websites that:

Are X-rated or have sexual content	44%
Have information about hate groups	25%
Teach how to build bombs	14%
Show where or how to buy a gun	12%

What do your parents know about the websites you visit?

A lot	38%
A little	45%
Nothing	17%

Do your parents have rules about your Internet use, and do you follow them?

Yes, and always follow	31%
Yes, but don't always follow	26%
No, parents don't have rules	43%

Have you ever encountered people online who:

You suspect are pretending to be someone they're not
YES   Girls 72%   Boys 57%
Say offensive things
YES   Girls 66%   Boys 54%
Want personal information like your address or phone #
YES   Girls 58%   Boys 39%

Gun Availability

Very few restrictions for gun availability in our country make guns accessible. Not only are guns readily available, but also automatic weapons, AK-47's, Uzi's, the kind that have big ammunition clips, the kind that can unload 10 or 20 rounds into a person in 10 or 20 seconds are available. Kids are getting these weapons. Sawed-off shotguns are also available. These are not hunting weapons. They are assault weapons. Why are they so available? 1,400 Americans are killed accidentally each year by guns.

50,000 handguns were in circulation in the late 1980s. One-half of the households in this country now contain guns, but guns do not stay where their owners put them. Kids brag about how easy it is to access guns. They take them out of their dad's closets or dressers. They can borrow them, steal them, or purchase them for $20.00.

How does gun availability impact our culture? According to statistics, the United States stands at the top of the list when you look at how many young men, aged 15-24, are killed each year.

Country	Killings per 100,000 men (1986)
Austria	0.3
Japan	0.5
England	1.2
France	1.4
Sweden	2.3
Australia	2.5
Canada	2.5
United States	21.9

Source: *Journal of the American Medical Association*

Guns were used in less than 25% of murders of young males in Europe and Japan. Guns were used in 75% of the homicides in the United States.

Country	Handgun Deaths in 1985
United States	8,092
Japan	46
Switzerland	31
Israel	18
Great Britain	8
Australia	5

Certainly, there are other factors in our culture that account for these figures besides gun availability. In Israel and Switzerland, almost every household has a gun, yet guns are not used to kill people very often. It is, however, interesting to compare homicide statistics for Seattle and Vancouver from 1980-1986. These cities are only 140 miles apart, are about the same size, and have the same rates of unemployment and average income. Seattle had 388 homicides during that time, while Vancouver had 204. In Seattle, where handguns are available, 139 people were shot to death. In Vancouver, with restrictive handgun laws, only 25 were shot to death during the same period.

Several summers ago, we were in northwest Colorado near the White River. We were staying in a cabin with friends. It is a beautiful spot. One night we went out to dinner in a rustic log cabin restaurant in the area. The meal was great, and everyone had a good time. As I was leaving, I looked at the outside of the building and noticed a sign. It stated, "This property protected by armed citizens." I couldn't believe it. The owners of the restaurant were willing to get their guns out to protect their restaurant, engage in a gun fight if need be, and all the while my wife and I would be sitting there eating. Needless to say, I felt uneasy. I probably would not eaten there if I had read the sign when I arrived. Gunfights at the O.K. Corral aren't just in the movies anymore.

In many of our cities, carrying a handgun is considered normal behavior for adults and also for kids. Even "good" kids feel compelled to carry guns for protection.

It makes sense to me to try to get guns out of the hands of kids. Preventing them from getting guns in the first place can best accomplish this objective. Parents have several choices. The first is obvious – don't allow guns in your home. For those who like to hunt and shoot for recreation, this option is tough. An alternative option is to keep guns locked up in a manner that kids cannot get them. This measure can be lifesaving. Because they had access to guns that went off, many kids are killed each year. For example, in Jacksonville recently, a 12 year old was accidentally shot and killed by his buddy who found a gun at home. As the two were playing, the gun went off.

Why automatic and semiautomatic weapons are available in our country remains a mystery. These are assault weapons that are designed to kill people. How do they end up in the hands of kids? Anything that is for sale at gun shows or gun shops gets in the hands of kids. That means these weapons are available to kids – our kids. These weapons should not be available to anyone. They should not be allowed on the streets. They should not be for sale anyplace.

Our culture is a violent one. It's so violent that we hardly notice. Littleton may have changed all that – this tragedy has somehow gotten our attention.

AMA STUDY ABOUT VIOLENCE

Just recently, August 9, 1999, the *Journal of the American Medical Association* printed an article entitled, "Recent Trends in Violence-Related Behaviors Among High School Students in the United States." Data was gathered in 1991, 1993, 1995, and 1997 through Youth Risk Behavior Surveys.

The data shows that males were significantly more likely than females to engage in each of the behaviors examined except feeling too unsafe to go to school.

Results of the
Journal of the American Medical Association

Survey of Violence-Related Behaviors Among
High School Students in the United States

	1991	1997	% change
Physical fighting	42.5%	36.6%	-14%
Students injured in fight	4.4%	3.5%	-20%
Students carrying weapon	26.1%	18.3%	-30%
Students carrying gun	7.9%	5.9%	-25%
Students fighting at school	16.2%	14.8%	-9%
Students carrying a weapon to school	11.8%	8.5%	-28%

Between 1991 and 1997, students were less likely to carry weapons, to engage in physical fights and to be injured in physical fights. The findings also indicated that between 1993 and 1997 students were less likely to carry guns but not other weapons, less likely to carry weapons on school property, and less likely to fight on school property. In each of the four survey years, the percentages of students carrying weapons on school property or fighting on school property were far lower than students carrying weapons or fighting when not on school property.

These findings suggest that adolescent violence is more of a generalized problem. School violence is just an extension of that problem. National health objectives for the year 2000 recognize that violence is not restricted to schools and is aimed at reducing weapon carrying and fighting in general and not just at school. Even though there has been a 31% decrease in weapon carrying from 1991 to 1997 and a 16% decrease in fighting, youth violence still remains alarmingly high. Hispanic students are not showing this trend, i.e., a decrease in weapon carrying and fighting. African-American and white students, however, are. Fighting between females has also decreased more than fighting between males during this same period of time.

The homicide rate among young people, aged 14 to 17 years, has also decreased steadily since 1993. The homicide rate in 1997 was at the lowest level since 1988. Despite these recent reductions, rates of youth homicide and perpetration of violence remain at historically high levels. Many kids, however, still feel unsafe at school. There have been reductions in gun carrying and fighting at school, and this statistic is encouraging, but there is still a lot of youth violence at school and away from it. This prevalence of violence is unacceptable. Not only is there a great physical and emotional toll from violence, but there also is a great financial cost as well.

In 1997, gunshots caused 31,636 fatal injuries and 100,000 nonfatal injuries in our country. In 1996, there were 134,445 gunshot injuries, with the cost per injury approximately $17,000. Thus, lifetime medical costs total $2.3 billion. $1.1 billion was paid by U.S. taxpayers. Insurance companies and other funding sources paid the remainder of the cost.

We are all involved directly and indirectly with the costs of shootings in the United States. Gunshot wounds overburden our inner city hospital emergency rooms. Our culture can dramatically cut into these costs if we are willing to take the steps. Gun availability can be controlled. Other countries, such as England, Japan, and Canada, are very successful in controlling gun availability. Their gunshot wound statistics prove this fact. Also, assault weapons are not available to anyone on the open market in these countries. Handguns are also restricted. These measures go a long way in protecting people from gunshot wounds, with their devastating consequences.

Are we, as a culture, willing to tolerate the pain and anguish that almost unrestricted gun control allows? Or are we willing to put up with tougher gun restrictions? From my point of view, the answers are obvious. We want safer schools, safer work places, and safer streets. Guns are just too easy to obtain.

12

What's Going on in Schools

The May 10th issue of *Time* magazine ran a Time-CNN poll of kids, aged 13-17.

How likely is it that an incident similar to the one in Littleton, Colorado would occur in your school?

Very or somewhat likely	33%
Not very likely or not at all likely	66%

Do you know someone your age who has talked about committing a serious act of violence at your school?
If so, did you tell an adult about it?

Yes, and told an adult	8%
Yes, and didn't tell an adult	13%
No	79%

How responsible are the following for shootings like the one in Colorado?

	Very/ Somewhat	Not Very/ Not At All
Availability of guns	87%	13%
Internet	75%	24%
Parents	67%	33%
Violence in movies, TV & music	66%	34%
Violence in video games	56%	43%
Violence in news	55%	44%

Before we disregard this survey, I think we need to understand that kids know who at their school is dangerous. They
know what is going on. I think of myself as someone who knows
something about what is going on in the adolescent subculture, but I was not aware of the extent of the violence or the
availability of guns.

How safe are schools? The most recent data comes from the
Annual Report on School Safety, 1998, published by the United
States Government, by the Department of Education and by
the Attorney General. Most schools are safe. More violent crimes
occur outside schools than inside. Although school homicides
are rare events, violence does occur in schools. As a culture,
we can't tolerate any school violence.

Among students, aged 12-18, 26 of every 1,000 were victims of serious violent crimes outside of school. 10 of 1,000
students were victims of serious violent crimes in school. In
1996, 5% of all 12th graders reported that they had been injured on purpose with a knife, gun, or club during the past
year while at school. 12% were injured on purpose without a
weapon. This number has been the same for 20 years. Less
than 1% of the more than 7,000 children who were murdered
in 1992 and 1993 were killed in school. During that time period, 65 students, aged 5-19, were murdered at school. School-
associated violent deaths declined during 1992-1993. However,
the number of multiple-victim homicide events has increased
from 2 in 1992-1993 to 6 in 1997-1998.

251 kids have died in schools since the 1992-1993 school year

State	Number
California	15
Colorado	14
Florida	14
Texas	13
Georgia	12
Washington, DC	11
New York	10
Pennsylvania	10
Illinois	9
Missouri	9

A small number of schools reported one or more violent crimes to the police during the 1996-1997 school year. Most commonly, these were fights without weapons. One-third of schools with more than 1,000 students reported crimes of violence, while one school in ten reported violence in schools with fewer than 1,000 students. City schools were twice as likely to report serious violent crimes as those in towns or rural locations were.

The presence of deadly weapons brought to schools has declined over the past few years. High school seniors were less likely to bring weapons to school, 6% in 1996, compared to 8% in 1993. The percentage of males carrying weapons to school dropped from 14% in 1993 to 9% in 1996. In the 1996-1997 school year, 6,093 students were expelled for taking guns to school.

We know that kids carry guns and bombs to school. We know that kids have access to guns and can find out how to build pipe bombs. We know that there are troubled kids at school. So, how can we keep schools safe?

The following ideas for eliminating violence from school are taken from the "National School Safety Center," a publication dated 10/26/98.

- Get rid of the "It can't happen here" mentality. Violence invades schools in rural areas, the suburbs and in urban areas.

- Practice information sharing. Train children to tell responsible authorities when they learn of threats of violence.

- Stay in touch with your children's schools. Support your children by attending school meetings, parent-teacher conferences, school programs and other activities.

- Volunteer to help in schools. The presence of responsible adults volunteering in schools makes a tremendous difference.

- Take part in parenting classes. Enroll in classes that provide training in developing coping skills for resolving conflicts with children and that provide training for shared problem solving.

- Counsel children. Discuss with children the violence that they see and feel. Children need to develop awareness skills for perceiving potential violent situations and for coping with the results of violent acts.

- Provide care and supervision for children and youth. Hire someone to look after kids until a parent arrives home from work.

- Enroll children and youth in after-school programs. Find an activity for your child: youth groups, scouting, Boys and Girls Clubs, sports teams, volunteer activities, etc. These opportunities help build self-esteem, among other benefits.

- Show respect for your children. Demonstrate unconditional love. Encourage your child to try new activities and to learn from mistakes.

- LISTEN to your children. "TALK with them – not just to them."

Although there are things we can do, there are other things that we cannot control. Guns go to school. They come through the doors, brought by kids. Guns are also found outside of schools. Since the mid-1970s, homicides by juveniles involving guns have increased threefold. During that same period, arrests of kids for weapons violations increased 117%. When kids make guns the weapons of choice, violence becomes deadly. About 1 in 20 (5%) of kids carry guns.

Where do kids get guns? According to the May 31, 1999, issue of *Time* magazine, most kids get guns at home.

WHO	WEAPON	WHERE OBTAINED
Barry Loukaitis	.30-.30-cal. rifle	home
Luke Woodham	.30-.30-cal. rifle	home
Michael Carneal	.22-cal. Ruger pistol	stolen from a neighbor
Andrew Golden Mitchell Johnson	3 rifles, 7 handguns	stolen from relatives
Kipland Kinkel	.22-cal. semiautomatic rifle, 2 pistols	presents from father
Eric Harris Dylan Klebold	handgun, rifle, 2 shotguns	some bought by friends, home
Thomas Solomon	.22-cal. rifle	home

Harris and Klebold also had a TEC 9 semiautomatic handgun along with 2 sawed-off shotguns. It doesn't make sense to allow guns to be available to kids unsupervised in our homes.

In August of 1998, law enforcement officials put on a seminar entitled *Lessons Learned: An FBI Perspective/School Violence Seminar* in Little Rock, Arkansas.

The discussion included the following proactive measures.

PROACTIVE MEASURES

Scholastic crime stoppers

Anonymous tips line/box where students can convey information

Establish a "zero" tolerance program for threats of violence by students, which means expulsion or suspension

School resource officers must provide positive information quickly and must weed out rumors quickly. They must develop ways to find out about potential or planned violence.

Patrol officers should be adopting schools in their beats and spending time at the schools, having lunch with students, getting to know them so that a trusting relationship is formed.

Develop a relationship between schools and police before any planning or training can be done.

Develop a crisis response team who will devise, with the police, a plan of action for a crisis situation.

The discussion also included the following preventative measures.

PREVENTATIVE MEASURES

Teachers, administrators, and counselors at schools need to be trained to recognize students at risk.

When students at risk are detected, parents, administrators, and counselors should be alerted.

Police should also be alerted if there is a potential for violence.

WARNING SIGNS THAT MAY PRECEDE VIOLENCE

A history of violence
A history of alcohol or drug abuse
A failed romance
Availability of weapons
Recent attempts of suicide or violence
Lack of coping skills
Anger
No apparent support systems

They learned that in all but one of the shootings, the violent kids talked about their plans to other kids. Kids in the school knew who the dangerous kids were and what they were about. The problem was that the kids who knew didn't tell anyone. They did not go to their teachers or to the police. In Littleton, Colorado, kids knew what was going on. In fact, the police were told that Klebold and Harris were dangerous, but no one acted on the information.

Somehow, kids need to easily get information to the right people, and, in turn, this information needs to be taken seriously. When students threaten other students, this terrorizing must be taken seriously and cannot be tolerated. Students who threaten should be suspended or expelled. There must be a zero tolerance for threats of killing or assaulting at every school. Intervention must be swift and decisive. When adults respond this way, students realize that violence will not be tolerated.

In some schools, students have formed crime stoppers organizations, which are groups of students who are sensitive to what is going on at the school and who have a way of reporting to teachers or other school officials. Other schools have an anonymous tips box or a phone-recording device where kids can express their concerns anonymously. I think teachers and administrators need to have planned meetings with students to keep on top of what is going on. Class officers, student council leaders, and other student leaders need to be involved. Lines of communication must be formed and kept open.

Furthermore, teachers and counselors at schools need to be trained to spot kids at risk. An effort should then be made to see what is going on. Teachers have the ability and means to establish and develop relationships with troubled kids. Most kids welcome a teacher's interest. Just a simple, "How are things going?" or "You look sad to me" can get a dialogue started. Teachers, however, are often too overworked or have too many students for this approach to be realistic. Kids tend to write how they feel and who influences them in their papers – clues can be found there. Somehow, we need to get to know kids, especially troubled ones.

The FBI report listed warning signs that help teachers spot troubled kids.

TROUBLED KIDS – WARNING SIGNS

A history of violence or preoccupation with violence (movies, video games, writing, and class comments).

A close family member who has committed a violent act.

A history of alcohol or drug use.

A precipitating event, such as a failed romance or teasing and taunting.

Availability of weapons or a means to commit violence.

Recent attempts to commit suicide or violence.

Anger, a lack of coping skills.

No apparent support system.

13

What We Learned from Littleton

We have just lived through a decade of school violence, deadly violence with guns, pipe bombs, and death. It's frightening to send our kids to schools that are not safe. What can we do to prevent these violent situations? Perhaps by looking at two kids, Dylan Klebold, 17, and Eric Harris, 18, we can get some answers to the very unsettling question about why the tragedy at Columbine High School happened. At times like these, it often seems easier to come up with simplistic answers to very serious and complicated problems. No simple answers exist. At least some of the answers, hopefully, are somewhat obvious.

Eric Harris grew up as a boy in Plattsburgh, New York, and seemed destined to become one of the kids that made the "in crowd" in his high school. He played baseball on the Little League team and got good grades in school. A friend remembers Harris as being "really nice, easygoing and kind of quiet." Harris's dad was an Air Force pilot for 20 years, until the early 1990s. The family lived in Michigan, New York, Ohio, Kansas, Washington, and Oklahoma. In 1993, Wayne Harris retired from the Air Force and moved his family to Colorado.

Eric Harris seemed excited about moving to Colorado. He was a Colorado Rockies fan. When he left Plattsburgh, however, he left two close friends behind, one was African-American and the other was Asian American. Both boys were good athletes. When Harris moved to Littleton, he met new friends, including Dylan Klebold.

Dylan Klebold was 6 feet, 3 inches, a tall, skinny kid who drove a beat-up BMW. He was involved with computers and in theatrical productions, which put him outside of the "in group" at Columbine High School. Thomas Klebold, Dylan's father, ran a mortgage management business. His mother, Susan, worked with handicapped students. They lived in a nice section of Littleton.

Klebold and Harris started hanging out together during their sophomore year. They went to the movies, played video games at arcades, or went bowling. As they became closer friends, Klebold's other friends noticed changes in him. Friends of Klebold watched these changes happen over time. First, there was the involvement with the computer kids. Then, it was the black clothing. Klebold and Harris belonged to their own group – they called themselves the Trench Coat Mafia. The kids in this group wore dark duster-style coats over black pants and shirts. The 1998 yearbook contains a picture of the Trench Coat Mafia posing together. They considered themselves "outsiders."

Finally, Klebold was going through the personality changes that you often see in troubled kids. For instance, he went from being outgoing and friendly to an angry, defiant young man who got into trouble with the law. The boys then involved themselves in Nazism and aggressive German techno bands such as Rammerstein. These changes had to be troubling to Klebold's family members who are Jewish. His mother's grandfather was a prominent figure in the Jewish community in Ohio. During this time, they were also interested in explosive devices and guns.

The "in" crowd at Columbine High School certainly did not accept Klebold and Harris. The two of them often commented on the attitude of the jocks whom they felt ran the school. Klebold and Harris, conversely, were into computers and drama. They were smart and creative – all this pushed them into a different adolescent subculture.

Because students picked on them, Klebold and Harris walked with their heads down through the halls of Columbine High School, wanting to get to the safety of their classrooms rapidly. Other students, particularly the athletes, taunted them, called them "fags," and shoved them into lockers. As such, Klebold and Harris became angry young men who obviously felt intimidated and powerless in this situation. "They hung around with their own little pod at school," said Eric Beck, 16, who shared a video production class with Harris and Klebold.

"They were smart kids, very creative. They used their imagination a lot."

Robin Muske, a sophomore at New Hampshire's Portsmouth High School, stated, "I totally understand. I think everyone has that moment when you think about killing someone." She describes herself as one who once was "one of the worst outcasts" in school. She didn't agree with what Harris and Klebold did, but she did understand how that could happen. She wasn't the only one who thought this way – other students who also felt pushed to the fringes of their peer groups could understand how this could happen.

C. Ronald Huff, an Ohio State University criminologist, who has studied youth violence for 13 years, states, "It's all about payback and with the easier availability of weapons, the conflicts have become more lethal. Most people who have been marginalized will make a reasonable adjustment to compensate. A smaller percentage will become violent, either to others or themselves." He believes that parents who don't involve themselves in their kids' lives are more responsible for violence than the violent entertainment media. He pointed out that Japan's movies and televisions are far more brutal than ours, while their society is far less so.

There were many signs that Harris and Klebold were troubled. In January of 1988, they were caught breaking into a van to steal about $500 worth of electronic equipment. The court made them get involved with a yearlong program aimed at helping kids who were arrested. Their supervisor was impressed to the extent that he let them leave the program early. Termination reports stated that Klebold was a bright young man who had a great deal of potential. His prognosis was good. It also stated that Harris was a bright young man who was likely to succeed in life. His prognosis was also good. The report came out at the end of March 1998. At the same time, Eric Harris was experimenting with pipe bombs at home. Both young men were told not to use "a firearm, destructive device or other dangerous weapon" for an entire year. The year ended March 25th of 1999.

As I read over the clues that Eric Harris and Dylan Klebold gave before the Littleton assault, I felt that this tragedy could have been averted. One sign occurred on July 4, 1998, when Harris and Klebold ran into classmate Peter Maher at a 7-Eleven.

After an exchange of words, they waved a pistol at Maher from the window of Klebold's BMW. Another clue also occurred in 1998 when Klebold and Harris made a video in which they pretended to shoot friends dressed as jocks. Another piece of evidence is Harris's profile on an America Online Web site that includes the quote "Kill'em AALLLL." Even before this, an English teacher brought the works of one of the boys to the attention of the guidance counselor because the writings were so violent. In 1999, at least one teacher and two parents reportedly warned authorities that these two boys were violent. On April 30, 1999, Harris came to school wearing a T-shirt that read Serial Killer. Later, after changing into all black, he advised a friend to leave school. Supposedly, Harris and Klebold constructed pipe bombs in their garages. Teachers knew these kids were dangerous. So did some parents of their classmates. Students knew it also. This knowledge was given to law enforcement agencies. The dangerousness of the situation was just not realized until it was too late. The clues, however, were there.

Many of these violent kids had other shared characteristics. For example, they were taunted, teased by their classmates, and they were considered different. An athlete teased Barry Loukaitis at his school. Barry shot him. Luke Woodham was called pudgy, gay. Michael Carneal was called gay in the school newspaper. Mitchell Johnson was teased for being fat. Eric Harris and Dylan Klebold were labeled Trench Coat Mafia, and were called faggots. These kids were taunted, teased, humiliated, and slammed against lockers. Schools cannot tolerate this type of behavior. Just the presence of teachers in the halls often stops a lot of this. Kids need to realize that they will be suspended if they engage in this kind of behavior.

Here are some clues that should raise red flags about boys.

Problems at School
- Skipping school
- Falling grades
- Defiant, angry behavior
- Unusual dress (black)
- Silver rings
- Being taunted, picked on
- Preoccupation with violence, guns

Problems with the Law
- Getting arrested
- Abuse of drugs and alcohol

Personality Changes
- Outgoing, friendly becomes alone, quiet, and withdrawn
- Irritability, anger
- Changes in appearance, dress, and hairstyles
- Talk about violence, murder, death, and suicide

I take adolescents seriously when they talk about suicide or violence. These comments should never be ignored. Adults should pick up on these signs. We cannot ignore statements about violence. What went on at Columbine High School was predictable. These two kids told anyone who was willing to listen that something dangerous was about to happen.

14

Keeping Schools Safe

How Safe are Schools?	
Homicides	Fewer than 1% of homicides involving school-age children occur in or around schools, according to figures from the Centers for Disease Control.
Shootings	Since 1992 the annual death toll from school shootings has ranged from 20 to 55, according to the National School Safety Center. In the last school year there were 40.
Theft	43% of the nation's schools had no crime at all in the 1996-97 school year, according to the Department of Education. The vast majority of incidents were minor crimes such as theft and vandalism.
Weapons	In 1997, 8% of high school students said they had carried a weapon to school in the preceding month. That was down from 12% in 1993.

How can we keep schools safe?

First, we, as parents and grandparents, must support public schools. More and more good teachers are leaving the profession. In Florida, teachers are not being paid enough. Often, they have to work two jobs to make ends meet. Classes are larger than they should be. It is hard to teach and maintain discipline in large classes. It is also hard to keep in touch with a lot of kids and know what is going on in their lives. Many students come from bad home situations. Teachers are called upon to spot and help these kids, but with so many kids, this is difficult. I am very impressed with the teachers my grandchildren have. They are great teachers and good people. They try hard, often in very difficult situations. I find, however, that teachers are becoming very discouraged.

How can we support teachers?
By getting to know them.
By joining the PTA.
By being a class mother or father.
By tutoring students who are behind.
By urging politicians to put more money into the school system.
By encouraging administrators to allocate more funds for
    teachers' salaries and for classroom use.
By getting involved.

So many of us denigrate public schools. We even call them "government schools," as a negative designation. These schools, however, are the ones where we send our kids and grandkids, where our friends and relatives send their kids, and where most of the parents in our nation send their kids. Sure, these schools have problems, but the solution is not found in abandonment but in support.

Spotting Troubled Kids Early
We need to help kids who have learning problems in the early part of the educational process. This means we have to identify kids who have trouble reading or doing math by the time they get to the first or second grade. Kids can be helped but they need to be identified and worked with early. Not doing well academically also brands these children as slow learners by their classmates. It is humiliating not to be able to read well aloud. It is hard to go to the blackboard and not be able to do the math problems. These children feel ashamed because they cannot do the work – their classmates consider them dumb.

Most of them, however, can learn with some help. Most of them want to learn; they were eager to learn the first day they came to school. There are many ways to solve this problem:

Hire class assistants.

Enlist volunteer moms and dads to tutor.

Appoint good students in higher grades to tutor.

Push for smaller class size.

I think I could go into most high schools, at least the suburban ones, and, in a few days, know who the troubled kids were. They are not that hard to spot. I think I would have spotted Dylan Klebold and Eric Harris as troubled kids. All one had to do was look at how they were dressed. I am sure their teachers knew that something was going on. I would have tried to get to know the Trench Coat Mafia kids. I would have eaten with them, talked to them, found out where they hung out. These kids need adults to come alongside, to listen to them, and to become friendly with them. Troubled kids need to be spotted and helped. Kids need mentors and role models – adults who will take the time to get to know them and establish a relationship with them. When I was involved in high schools in the 1960s and 1970s, kids were very easy to get to know. All I had to do was remember their names. I do not think I ever felt rejected by any of them. They were friendly, willing to talk and very accepting. Often they asked me why I hung around their high school. I might add that I still have contact with these friends of mine, even after many years.

Parental Involvement

Parents also need to be in close contact with teachers. They need to know if their kids are having trouble academically. Kids tend to say everything is fine, that their grades are good. Then report cards come out and grades are not good. By that time, parents are upset and kids are discouraged. Being successful in school is not rocket science. It has to do with completing assignments, doing the work correctly, and handing it in on time. It also has to do with good study habits. Most kids cannot do well if they put off studying for a test until the night before or on the way to school in the morning. There needs to be designated study time – 2 or 3 hours daily, including weekends. Studying is best done at the kitchen or dining room table, where parents can see what's going on, with no television, radio, or phone calls. Parents need to know what's assigned by teachers and they need to inspect the assignments to make sure the work is done and done well. Parents need to take an active role in this aspect of their child's life.

Should kids finish their work, but for some reason not hand it in, then this could be due to the disorganization of ADHD, learning disabilities, or just the fact that it's not cool to do homework. For whatever reason, parents need to be on top of any problem.

It makes sense for parents to be actively involved in their kid's learning at an early age. Sometimes, however, everything goes well until the 7th or 8th grade, and then things go downhill fast. Parents need to jump in at that time and know what's going on. Kids need to be structured. It's easy for many kids to do well in elementary school with very little effort. This changes during middle school or high school. Classes get harder and kids need to be disciplined and structured, often producing conflict between parents and kids. Kids want freedom; parents want discipline. Remember, the chief goal of parenting is not to be a friend or buddy of your adolescents, but to help them find structure and discipline in their lives so that they will become responsible, caring adults. Part of that process includes disciplined study habits. Kids should not be turned loose before they become responsible. They need encouragement, help, and structure to make it through the time of adolescence. They need our involvement. They may resent it, but they need it.

Police Involvement

School resource officers, those officers permanently assigned to the school by the police department, need to follow up on rumors quickly and must act on the rumors that are potentially dangerous. These officers must find ways to invade the high school community so that kids will tell them what is going on. They need to hang out with the students and eat lunch with them. Establishing lines of communication and keeping them open are essential.

Likewise, the police and schools must establish a relationship before any training or planning can be done. Schools need to develop a crisis response team, which needs to work with the police. This team can develop a plan that is appropriate for that particular school. The police can educate teachers and school administrators as to what is going on in the community regarding gangs, drugs, and violence. Graffiti, literature, music and other art forms correlate with gangs and cults. Music, video games, and movies that depict violence have a huge impact on a small number of kids. The police can also help identify troubled kids. Generally, offenders display certain traits that the police and teachers can pick up. Violent kids make statements about what they are going to do. The problem then becomes how to get this information to the school authorities and to the police. Certainly, a scholastic crime stoppers program with a tip line would enable kids to get information to adults anonymously. Had this program been in place, some of the violence our schools experienced could have been avoided.

In areas where there are a lot of gang activities and drugs, especially in the inner cities, schools need to be monitored. It may make sense to have kids go through metal detectors. You would hope that schools would be safe without this type of supervision, but that may be unrealistic. I would hate to see schools become like prisons, but that may become reality. The bottom line remains – schools must be safe. You do whatever is necessary to accomplish this purpose.

Can we make schools safer? I think so, but all of us need to help. We need to get involved. Schools need to be places where children learn, where they feel safe and secure. Schools need to be places where teachers, principals, and administrators feel safe, where they can teach and run schools. Right now, it is hard to be a teacher. It is hard to be a principal in many schools. We have to support our schools. We need to support teachers and principals. We need to get involved.

Bullying – Zero Tolerance

Schools should not tolerate bullying, taunting, or intimidating. No child should have to go to school and be picked on every day. We know that this goes on in our schools. Kids who are teased feel humiliated and defenseless. We know that Eric Harris and Dylan Klebold were harassed repeatedly by their classmates. Bullies are a problem in every school. Everyday, they make certain kids feel uncomfortable. The National Association of School Psychologists estimates that 160,000 kids miss school every day because of bullying. As many as 7% of eighth graders stay home from school every month because of bullying.

To address bullying, many schools offer a "bullyproof" program. Kids start by learning what a bully is and how a bully behaves. They learn what a bully looks for in his/her victim. Students then learn how to diffuse the situation when bullies approach them. Anyone involved in bullying is warned the first time. If that does not work, then the bully must face stiffer consequences. Bullying can not be tolerated.

Often the first experience young boys have with violence comes at school through bullying. This starts early, first or second grade, even in kindergarten. Bullies learn early that physical violence is not tolerated at most elementary schools. But bullies find other ways, such as taunting, insulting, jeering, and threatening, to intimidate and shame.

Jim was in the 2nd grade. He was a young second grader, small for his age, and had just moved to the city with his family. He did not know anyone at school and felt isolated and alone when he was there. Although he had met several kids that he liked, there was one boy named Charles who picked on him. Charles was one of the older kids in the second grade who was bigger than the other boys and was always the first boy chosen for sports. He went out of his way to pick on Jim by calling him "new boy." Charles also ridiculed Jim for being small and for being picked last for kickball. In general, he made it very uncomfortable for Jim. After awhile, the situation got so bad that Jim started to have a headache and an upset stomach every morning before school. Jim's mom was concerned about the entire situation. She knew that Charles was the problem, but she wasn't sure how to handle it. Finally, she went to Jim's teacher about the problem. Not much happened. Jim's mom and dad tried to help him deal with it, but the problem remained. It was hard for Jim to go to school. He was in a constant state of uneasiness. Finally, Jim's parents confronted Charles's parents, and the bullying stopped.

In middle school or high school, other strategies can be used to curb bullying. For example, principals and assistant principals, coaches, and teachers need to invade the adolescent subculture. They need to walk through the halls of their schools and find out what is going on with the kids who attend there. Just the presence of adults in the halls and in the lunchroom can diffuse a lot of the intimidating that's going on. Kids are reluctant to taunt or intimidate their classmates when adults are around.

Schools will always have cliques. Teachers and staff need to know which students are part of the "in" crowd and which ones are excluded. They also need to know who is being picked on. It seems that athletes do a lot of taunting. Athletes tend to be popular and cool. They need to know that taunting, teasing, and intimidating will not be tolerated. Coaches need to work with their athletes to make sure that they understand and comply. Athletes get the idea that they have to be "macho." Often, their behavior has been ignored, even encouraged.

Some ways to address the bullying issue include:

Form peer facilitator groups.

Improve communication among teachers, principals, and students.

Teach tolerance to students.

Establish student courts.

Peer facilitator groups that mix different students together are helpful. When kids are allowed to get to know each other, they often break down barriers. This model was successful in the 1970s when my oldest daughter was in high school. It brought kids together who otherwise would have never interacted. Different kids started to understand each other and learned to respect one another.

A closer connection among teachers, principals, and students needs to be fostered. Kids involved in different interest groups (e.g., band, athletics, student government, computer clubs) need to meet regularly with teachers and principals. Kids know what is going on in their school. If 50 students were asked who the dangerous kids in school are, the same students would show up on almost every list. Kids know who the bullies are.

We need to teach kids tolerance. Because we live in a pluralistic society, one that contains many different groups, we have to be tolerant and get along. Tolerance needs to be learned at home, as well as at school. Intolerance just cannot be tolerated. Intolerant behavior needs to be looked for, intercepted, and stopped. Students need to know that being intolerant has consequences. Schools that have established student courts have been successful in stamping out some intolerance. Kids are stricter on their classmates than adults sometimes are.

Weapons in School

Weapons come to school. They come through the doors – in backpacks, pockets, and even lunch boxes. Kids carry guns, knives, pipe bombs to school. Can we keep weapons out of our schools? Yes, but with great difficulty. Kids get guns from home, relatives, friends, and neighbors. I've never had a gun in my house; my daughters were not exposed to them. This stance, however, is unrealistic. Guns will be in homes. The problem is how to keep them out of the hands of kids. There are ways to make guns less accessible to kids: locking them up, deactivating them, separating them from ammunition, and storing them outside the home.

What else can be done? The Brady bill requires an instant background check when someone purchases a gun from a licensed dealer. This law has kept hundreds of thousands of felons, fugitives, those dishonorably discharged from the military, and those with records of domestic violence from getting guns. These folks, however, can obtain guns through a secondary market: at private sales and from gun shows. Often, guns change hands with no record of sale. It is estimated that 40% of gun sales go through the secondary market. In almost every state, anyone can sell firearms at gun shows or at flea markets without conducting a background check on the buyer.

Assault weapons need to be banned. In 1994, there was a federal ban placed on assault weapons. The manufacturers just modified their models slightly to get around the law and put them back on the market. Is there any reason to have these weapons legitimately available? Ultimately, they end up in our homes and in the hands of kids. It makes sense to ban assault weapons.

Should we license owners and register all guns? This idea makes some sense. To drive a car, we have to demonstrate that we can drive. To own a gun, we should have to demonstrate that we can handle it safely. Also, if a gun is registered in one's name, then that owner would be more reluctant to pass that gun on to someone he/she does not know or is unsure of – maybe preventing some felons from getting guns.

Gun control is a complex problem, but one that we need to address. Our country is losing too many young males in our schools and on the streets because of gun availability. Without saying, schools must enforce a no guns, no knives policy. Kids cannot bring these weapons to school. Teachers and principals who walk the halls and know what is going on often keep weapons out of the schools just by their presence. This means knowing who kids are and knowing who would probably bring these weapons to school. Schools must be kept safe – weapon free. If this means metal detectors or policemen on campus, so be it.

School Size

It also seems that bigger is not better. When it comes to schools, 2,000 or more students in one school is just too many. We need smaller schools and smaller classes. Somehow teachers need to know students better. This is hard to do when there are so many of them. Smaller schools have less crowding and less competition for memberships in choirs, band, student government, sports teams, and other activities. Through these activities, kids often express and define themselves. In smaller schools, more kids can get involved. It is not just the elite few.

At bigger schools, only a few kids can play in the band or make the football team. The competition is often brutal. When you do not make the team, you feel like a nobody. Every kid needs a chance to succeed, to feel like a "somebody." Small schools help bring about that feeling.

The small school movement is already underway in Chicago, New York, and Los Angeles. These cities have recently opened high schools of only 500 kids. They have even divided big schools into smaller schools, schools within schools. Studies already show that students get better grades in smaller schools. There is also less fighting and less gang involvement, because more adults are around watching. Kids are more willing to discuss problems with their teachers. The attendance is better, and the dropout rate is lower. Moreover, more kids participate in extracurricular activities. Things are just better in smaller schools. Shy kids, poor kids, and average athletes are made to feel that they fit in and that they are "somebody."

Small schools, equipped with full facilities and sports teams cost more per student than larger schools. But in the long run, they help kids not only survive, but also grow in their high school experience. Kids grow and develop when given opportunities to participate. Small schools give kids this chance.

Just recently, the Louisiana legislature came up with a new school language curriculum. Kids must say, "Yes, ma'am" and "Yes, sir" when talking to teachers and principals. That is not all bad. It mandates at least the outward appearance of respect. In the 1960s, kids said, "Yes, sir" to me, until they got to know me, and then it was "Doc." When the "Yes, sir" was abandoned, I knew that I was accepted. What adolescents really need is more adults in their lives – adults who will spend the time to find out what is going on and who will listen. They need adults who will invade their subculture and build relationships with them.

A publication called "Creating Safe and Drug-Free Schools, An Action Guide" lists some ways in which schools can ensure discipline and safety. (The United States Department of Education puts out this information.)

Establish a team of educators, students, parents, law enforcement and juvenile justice officials, and community leaders to develop a plan for creating a safe school.

Develop a Safe School plan based upon an examination of problems and resources and a review of strategies that work.

Ensure that students are engaged in schoolwork that is challenging, informative, and rewarding. (When students are fully absorbed, they are less prone to violence.)

Establish, publish, publicize, and enforce policies that clearly define acceptable and unacceptable behavior, including zero tolerance for weapons, violence, gangs, and use of alcohol and drugs.

Work with law enforcement and juvenile justice agencies for support in delinquent or criminal behavior.

Take immediate action on all reports of drug use or sales, threats, bullying, gang activity, or victimization.

Create an environment that encourages parents to visit the school and participate in the school's activities. Develop a sense of community within the school.

Encourage staff to treat each other and students with respect and to act as good role models.

Encourage community members to support schools in their community and to participate in school programs and services that promote the safety of students and all school staff.

Work with community groups and law enforcement officials to keep schools open after normal operating hours so that students and their families have places where they can engage in productive, well supervised, and safe activities.

Involve youth in program and policy development.

Offer programs that teach peaceful, nonviolent methods for managing conflict to students and their families, as well as to staff.

Provide accurate assessments of school crime and violence to the public.

Learn about effective practices based on research and proven programs used in other districts. Share the knowledge.

Monitor implementation and progress of the Safe School Plan, making improvements based on what is learned, as well as on new developments in the field.

Even though our schools are in crisis, there are many teachers who still teach and do an excellent job under very trying and stressful situations. There are good principals and administrators who know what goes on at their schools, who walk the halls and get to know their students. In this country, every day, three children die from child abuse and nine in car accidents. More kids suffer violence outside of schools than inside. As a matter of fact, most schools are safe havens for some children. We need to keep it that way and strive to keep schools even safer.

15
Changing Our Culture

Although we talk about gun control and violence on television and in the media, the basic questions remain: What's going on in our culture and what's happening to us as individuals? Our culture reflects who we are as people. Although, I'm bothered by what's been happening in our schools, I'm also bothered about what I see in me. More than I like to admit, I feel intolerance toward people with different lifestyles and backgrounds. I'm intolerant. Do my grandkids pick this up? I hope not, but I'm not sure. I laugh at ethnic jokes and put-downs. I'm capable of taunting, saying mean things. Deep inside me I also harbor anger – enough anger to make me wonder if I could control it in certain situations. Anger turned to rage is dangerous, potentially lethal. I look at myself as a giving, caring person, but I'm not so sure this is how I am. In a crunch, I'm interested in my needs being met, my ideas used, and my way. My profession calls our culture narcissistic and self-centered. Am I different?

Cassie Bernall, 17, lost her life at Columbine when she said she believed in God. This young lady found out, the summer before, that she needed something in her life, something radical, and something transforming. She was into drugs, ran around with the wrong crowd, and was even into witchcraft. At 16, she knew something was very wrong and that she needed to change. This happened at a Christian camp in the summer of 1998. Cassie became a Christian. The transformation was radical. Cassie found new friends, got involved with a Bible study, stopped doing drugs, and got out of witchcraft. The change was so profound that when she faced death and was asked if she believed in God, she answered, "Yes."

What happens when we program God out of our lives and out of our culture? I don't mean praying in school or hanging the Ten Commandments on the walls of public buildings. I mean programming God out of our lives and living our lives as if God doesn't exist or, if He does, acting as if He's somewhere off in the distance not interested in us.

For me, having God in my life changes me. It's not so much that I'm changed because I'm fearful of what will happen to me, but because I want to please the one I worship out of love, respect, and gratitude. I want to live a life that reflects His love and His involvement with me.

I'm a lot like Cassie, at least in some respects. I knew at a young age that something was wrong and that I needed change, radical transformation. I've been in this process a long time. I still need radical transformation and change after all these years. I'm not the person I want to be. I still act insensitively, still demand my own way, still get angry, and still take advantage of people. But because of conversion, I treat people differently. I'm more sensitive, less self-centered, more in control of my anger, and less prejudiced. In addition, I find meaning and purpose in my life when I live it as if God exists.

In our culture, life is not very valuable. Every day, kids are killed, one at a time, in drive-by shootings, in inner city neighborhoods, and accidentally while playing with guns. Columbine-like events happen every day – kids are killed violently. Why does our culture tolerate this violence? In other cultures, this violence doesn't exist. The only real difference between Canada and the United States is gun availability. Yet we do not have gun laws that keep guns out of the hands of kids. We can change that politically. The NRA, 3% of our population, controls gun legislation with money. 3% of the population controls the safety of our kids. Something seems wrong with that fact.

Several years ago, I clipped a memoriam out of the Jacksonville, Florida paper, from a grandmother to a grandson. It read:

October 7, 1975 – May 1994

Thinking of you on this day, your 20th birthday, brings back memories of yesterday. The thoughts of your laughter, the kindness, your caring and your sharing.

You were a special and a good grandson, your presence is absent and I miss you so much that sometimes it's almost unbearable, but your memories and love will be with me forever.

You'll always be precious to me.

Love, Grandmother

This young man had been shot.

This is what guns do in the hands of kids. Should we continue to allow this violence? Should we pay this kind of price for the lack of gun control? I think not. This is not sentimentality; this is reality. Every day, young men are being gunned down. Every day, grandmothers cry.

Violence is tolerated in the media also. Movies, videotapes, television shows, and computer games are so violent. They desensitize our kids to killing and to blood. We should be outraged. Movies like *Basketball Diary* are not only tolerated but their stars are idolized. There is no justifiable reason for movies like this – they exploit violence to make money at the box office. They also show kids how to shoot up their schools.

At the very heart of tolerance for violence, taunting, prejudice, and putting people down, I stand. I need transformation; I need to change. After completing this section, I found myself intolerant and demanding at the downtown inner city hospital where I work. Sometimes it is hard to work there. At times, I deal with situations that seem impossible, and I reveal my real self. I need conversion every day. I need to look at myself and change, or I pass this endless cycle of intolerance and hatred on to my grandchildren. If we didn't look at ourselves, realize how we really are and change, then not much would ever improve. Ten years from now, schools would still be terrorized, grandmothers would still cry, and kids would still be gunned down in the streets.

So, where does this conversion start? Where does change begin? It would seem that it has to start first in our families. Of the nine kids who were involved in school shootings, four of them came from broken homes. That's not all that surprising – 1 out of 2 marriages in our culture end in divorce. Do we really realize the effect divorce has on our children? I'm not sure.

It's a fact of life that divorce affects millions of kids everyday. Even in families that are together, kids come in contact with families whose mom and dad are divorced, or are going through a divorce. Several years ago, when children were asked in a survey what their greatest fear was, the most frequent answer was that a parent would die or that their parents would divorce.

Dr. William Pollack feels that divorce is the third trauma of boyhood. The first being the separation of boys too early from their moms; the second being the separation of teen-aged boys from their families during adolescence. Divorce disconnects kids from their parents. And somehow, kids feel guilty, as though they caused the divorce. They experience feelings of sadness, loss, and loneliness. Most boys live with their moms and many rarely or never see their dads. For a boy, divorce is a traumatic disconnection, usually from his dad. A boy's relationship to his mom also changes. She's more often than not, back in the work force, trying to be a good parent, trying to be both mom and dad, and often stressed out. There's little time left for him. As a result, sons feel that they have lost the safety and security of their home and family – their lives have been torn apart.

Marriage is for adults; it's not playing house together. Adults, supposedly, leave behind the self-centeredness of adolescence. They abandon the idea that marriage is where they get all their needs met. But we don't. Over and over again, I've been told, "She doesn't meet my needs." "He doesn't satisfy me." "I don't feel love anymore."

Marriage is more than getting our needs met; it's even more than having a loving feeling all the time. As a matter of fact, it's more of making a commitment that lasts a long time – a commitment that has to do with staying with another person for a lifetime – respecting, caring for, honoring, and loving forever. I need to be converted to this way of thinking consistently. I want feelings of love and excitement. I want my needs met, but this is an adult world we live in, not a kid's world.

Marriage is not for kids; it's for adults. Unfortunately, many adults agewise are still adolescents emotionally. They have yet to learn about delayed gratification, commitment, persistence, struggle, and work. Marriage requires maturity – it's not easy and it's not for kids.

If our culture is not converted, marriages ten years from now will be as unstable as they are today. How do we change this direction? Dads, love your children's mom. Make up your mind to respect her and to honor her. Same for moms – love your children's dad. Hang together and work on your marriage. Model for your kids what a giving, loving relationship is all about. Think about marriage as a lifetime commitment and show your kids how this is done.

A sign at a marina in Louisville, Kentucky, on the Ohio River reads, "Whoever dies with the most toys wins." We laugh, but many of us behave as though this outlook motivates us. Our kids need us, not the toys we provide for them. As a matter of fact, as I look back at my kids' childhood, I realize that probably the worst thing I provided for them was affluence. As I see my grandkids live in affluence, I hope and pray they survive it.

Time is our most valuable possession. Yet, most families think that what is needed is affluence. Often, both parents work, and kids are on their own after school. Moms and dads are not home when kids need them. Kids are demanding. Is it better for me to be the best psychiatrist possible or spend more time with my kids and grandkids? In theory, this choice is easy; however, how I behave reveals something else. The most important thing I can do is to involve myself with my grandkids. I know that. I need to spend more time with them. I don't see how parents who work, dads often 70 hours a week, get enough time for their kids.

We don't need all the toys we want. Our kids need our time, and so do our spouses. Priorities always boil down to time and how we spend it. If we don't prioritize our time, we will use it up on matters that are just not that important.

Today, I was walking to the hospital after parking my car. A colleague walked up to me and said, "You gave me some great advice a few years ago about my son. I was having difficulties with him and asked you what to do. You told me to hang out with him and spend time with him. You know, that was great advice. He's 16, a good kid, and we have a great relationship. I'll never forget what you told me." Hanging out and spending time together does work.

I have used the word conversion throughout this book. What does this term express? Conversion basically means to change your mind, to go in another direction. Usually, it is used in a religious way, but it doesn't have to be. Conversion means change – how one perceives things, how one thinks, how one behaves. We all need conversion, change, and new ways of thinking. If we don't, our culture will be worse ten years from now. We have to change – it's imperative.

Wouldn't it be great if our schools were safer and improved? They can be – it is just a matter of priorities. We need to get behind our public school system and support our teachers, principals, and administrators. In addition to not paying teachers fair wages, we put them in impossible situations, e.g., large classes, dangerous circumstances, and disrespectful students. Teachers risk physical assault and sometimes, even being shot. Most school systems are underfunded. Although money does not solve every problem, it could help solve class size and school size. Research proves smaller is better. Higher salaries would also attract more qualified candidates into the teaching profession.

We can make schools safer also. It's safer to ride on an airplane than it is to attend school. Metal detectors keep guns off airplanes – they could keep guns out of schools. School uniforms could keep kids who are not going to school off the campus. The presence of adults at the front doors and in school halls would cut down the taunting, fighting, and intimidation. More high school counselors would mean help for troubled kids.

Can we, as a culture, tolerate the availability of guns and the media violence that has become part of our lives? Can we tolerate drive-by shootings, gangs, drugs, and guns that shoot 20 rounds as fast as one can pull the trigger? I don't think so. We can stop these risks, but we need to take a pro-active stance. Politicians don't vote for stronger gun control because they don't think we care. Maybe they are right. We need to be converted. I don't want my grandkids exposed to the violence they see in video games, movies, and television. Can this violence be controlled? Can we, as human beings, tolerate a violent culture? Has the tragedy of Littleton told us anything at all? Is it really "noon in the garden of good and evil," or is it really closer to midnight?

Once again, I looked into the faces of twelve kids and one teacher – all filled with aspirations and hope, the joy of expectation, of life, of teaching. Once they were all alive, with us. Now they're gone – killed by two kids, classmates, students. We ask why. How could this tragedy happen? The answers are too simple, not really answers. We have to struggle with this one, and look deep inside ourselves. We also need to be converted and go in a new direction. Most of all, we need radical transformation, not only as individuals, but also as a culture. If we don't change, these terrible events will continue. So will the Columbine tragedy that goes on in our inner cities every day. If our culture is to change, we have to change at a deep level, where intolerance, hate, anger, and prejudice reside. We are a lot like Cassie – we need to change and be radically transformed.

16
Lost Boys

Many of the acts of violence committed by boys are deliberate rather than on the spur of the moment rage reactions. Some are planned meticulously. This intent points to the fact that some boys consider acts of violence as a way of solving their problems, implying that they feel they have been treated unfairly.

Michael Carneal, in Paducah, Kentucky, planned his attack while students were at a morning prayer meeting at their high school. In Arkansas, 13-year-old Mitchell Johnson and 11-year-old Andrew Golden drew students out of school by setting off a fire alarm. Eric Harris and Dylan Klebold had elaborate plans to attack students at Columbine High School. They even made a video about how they would do it.

What produces this frustration, this rage, which would cause these kids to attack? James Gilligan, in his book, *Violence: Our Deadly Epidemic and Its Causes*, believes that injustice produces shame and that shame in teens produces the intolerability of existence. Nothing seems to threaten us more than rejection, shame, and lack of love – these affect us at a very deep level.

Those who are abandoned, shamed, and rejected are vulnerable to acts of violence. How else does one "get even"? How else does one "settle a score"? Adolescents often see themselves as actors on a stage. Not only are they actors, but they are also the stars in the production. They act rashly and impulsively. Adolescents think they're invincible and that the world somehow revolves around them. Certainly, the acts of violence have placed adolescents at center stage. Their performances capture our attention.

Boys who grow up fatherless feel abandoned. They feel they have lost their protector, guide, mentor – the one male who should be there for him. The questions they ask are obvious, "How come I don't have a father?" and "What's wrong with me?" There is a strong connection to delinquency with these kids.

The same thing happens when mothers leave the family when sons are young. This abandonment, often considered deliberate abandonment by children, evokes a deep sense of shame in boys – the shame of rejection. This rejection often spills out into the world as anger, rage, and violence. Kids who lose a parent feel that their absent parent doesn't want them. They feel unattached and disjointed. These kids have trouble with their own feelings and the feelings of others. They have problems with empathy, sympathy, and caring. This disruption affects the child's ability to form secure, positive social relationships.

Often, these troubled young men feel no hope for the future; they see no way out. They also tend to lack purpose and meaning in their lives. They are like ships adrift, going in no particular direction.

Kids need meaning in their lives, but, as a culture, we have programmed it out. Victor Frankl endured the hardship of a Nazi concentration camp and, from this experience, wrote the classic book *Man's Search for Meaning*. He states that our search for meaning is a primary force in our lives. If our lives lack meaning and purpose, what happens when we are abandoned, rejected, and treated unjustly? Frankl got through his concentration camp experience because he found purpose and meaning in his life.

Bert Cohler, from the University of Chicago, states that having a coherent, meaningful account of one's life is a crucial factor in predicting how one makes it through the struggles of life. He maintains that life has to be organized and have meaning and purpose, if it is to make any sense at all to us.

Kids perceive purpose if their world makes sense. It makes sense to follow rules if you feel that the "rule makers" have your interest at heart. It makes sense to respect your elders if you see them well-intentioned and loving toward you. It makes sense to work hard and study if this effort is rewarded. It makes sense to be loving and kind if you have been treated this way. It makes sense to care for people if you and the people you care for are connected to each other within a positive spiritual order. If a boy's world doesn't make sense, then he feels adrift, with no purpose and no meaning. How does a boy cope with the feelings of being rejected and not being loved? How does he make sense out of life? Where does he find meaning and purpose for his life? Without the feeling of love, acceptance, and being part of a caring community, his life is reduced to a biological state. "I'm born, I live, I die."

There are several alternatives in how one thinks about this outlook. The first is: I'm born; life is O.K. Another is: I'm born; life sucks; I die. For many violent boys, life sucks. Dr. James Garbarino asked Tommy, who killed a police officer, "What have you learned from life?" Tommy answered, "Life sucks."

Dr. Garbarino goes on to state, "Spirituality and love can fill the holes left in a boy's life and help him develop both a strong positive sense of self and healthy limits. Religion can infuse life with purpose by connecting the ups and downs of everyday life to something permanent and beyond the reach of day-to-day experiences."

Psychologist Lloyd Wright is among a growing number of professionals who are looking at the role of religion and spirituality in helping adolescents cope with life. They find that if a depressed kid has a religious purpose in his life, it helps him with his depression. These young people attended church twice a month and felt that religion answered "many of the questions about the meaning of my life." They also claimed that religion played an important role in how they approached life.

Psychologist Andrew Weaver found that spirituality had a stabilizing effect on kids. He found they were less likely to attempt suicide and less likely to think about it. He also found that they did not suffer as much from depression and when they did, they were less depressed. Also, they were not as sexually active, and they waited longer before becoming so. Furthermore, these kids felt more support when they experienced trauma in their lives and recovered faster. And they were less likely to use drugs or alcohol.

There is good evidence that religion helps kids better cope with their parent's divorce. These kids trust God for protection and turn to Him for guidance.

It's interesting that Cornell and Harvard are finding out that adolescent boys who are religious have an easier time getting through adolescence and aren't as involved in problematic or dangerous situations. Religion does more than protect these young men from danger. It also gives them hope for the future, something to work for. And it provides meaning and purpose in life for kids. Although religious kids do have problems, research shows that religion is a stabilizing influence in the lives of many adolescents.

So, how do we react to this type of information? Many of us have come out of religious backgrounds. We were involved in churches or synagogues when we were kids. Some of us are still active in them. Others of us go on occasion, to special religious services. And some of us aren't involved at all. Let me encourage you to revisit your spiritual roots. Getting involved in religion gives your kids a structure that can help them make sense out of life. If we are just biological organisms, then "we are born, we live, we die." For an adolescent, that way of thinking doesn't offer meaning or purpose in life. In college, I read existential philosophy, which advocated, "Meaning can be found in life by just trying. We all fail, but in trying, we find meaning and purpose." I couldn't accept that. How could trying and failing bring meaning and purpose? Within the religious framework, we find possible answers to the great questions of life. Who am I? Where am I going? Does life have any purpose? Our kids need to be exposed to this thinking. So do we. We need to look once more at our religious upbringing and reconsider how important a religious background would be to our kids and also to us as parents. I'm not talking about the act of attending church on Sunday or the synagogue on Friday evening and then the rest of the time living as though God doesn't have any role in our lives. I am talking about active involvement, a real connection. Needless to say, boys need these anchors that protect them in the seas of adolescence.

Furthermore, boys need someone who loves them unconditionally, no strings attached. Hopefully, this person(s) is a family member, usually a mother and father, but could be a grandmother, grandfather, aunt or uncle. This love has to do with being born into the world, just arriving and being cared for. Kids are really fortunate to have more than one person who loves them unconditionally, whom they respond to and trust.

Some kids do not have family members who can or will provide this love for them. They need others outside the family to step in and offer this kind of relationship. They need mentors who will come alongside of them.

What qualities are needed in the persons who provide this kind of relationship for kids? First is unconditional love – the kind that accepts a person, not because they are perfect or talented, but because they exist and have value as a person. Does this mean that anything goes, that any behavior on the boy's part is overlooked? I don't think so. We can't overlook bad behavior. We have rules that everyone must live by. But we don't abandon someone because of bad behavior or failures. Kids need to grow and develop; they need to learn. Although they make mistakes during this process, they need adults who will love them and come alongside them to help and guide them.

Kids need to know adults who have their interests and their viewpoints at heart, one who is an advocate for them and will protect them when they get into difficult situations. Kids need to know that no matter what, they won't be abandoned and that they have a secure, safe place.

To take another person's point of view means taking the time to listen. To reiterate, empathetic listening is being able to put yourself in another person's situation and being able to feel, at least to some extent, what they are going through. Empathetic listening requires unhurried leisure, the feeling that you have the time to listen and that you are not rushing through, in a hurry to go somewhere else.

Kids need adults whom they can admire and who have their lives together. They need adults who have discovered that life is a great adventure with meaning and purpose, worth living. That doesn't mean, however, that the adult has a perfect life with everything figured out. Kids also need to be exposed to an adult's vulnerable side and realize that adults are sometimes discouraged and disappointed – that everything doesn't always go the way they want.

In addition, kids need a social network beyond their own families. They need to be part of a broader community, one that accepts them and cares for them, e.g., schools, churches, synagogues, athletic teams, Boy Scouts, Young Life. It takes more than a family, even the best of families, to get boys safely through adolescence. Families need all the help they can get, especially when biological families are spread out all over the place. My daughter's swim coach really helped her when we

moved from Gainesville, Florida, to Louisville, Kentucky, during her junior year of high school. This move was a tough one
for her, and her coach helped her in a way I couldn't.

Kids thrive in stable environments. They need stable families and they need parents who remain together and remain
connected to them. Kids need to know that their family is stable
and that their parents will be there for them. They also need to
know that there are other social institutions that they can count
on and that they feel a part of.

Not all boys have this type of stability in their lives. Many
troubled kids fall into this category. Denver has a mentoring
program that tries to address this problem. More than 600 men
mentor troubled boys. They take time for them, listen to them,
and love them. They provide the support that these young men
need during adolescence. What a great idea! Although mentoring
helps adolescents, it also provides men with the opportunity to
be involved in another person's life in a significant way.

Adolescence is still a difficult time for our sons. So many
different factors influence them. It's a confusing time for them.
They need the help and direction that adults can give them. We
need to be the kind of adults that take the time to get involved
with them, that come alongside of them, and help them make it
through the turbulent seas of adolescence.

17
Hope

Is there any hope for us as a culture? Is there any hope for us as individuals? Can we change? Can we go in a different direction? I think so.

Dads are spending more time with their sons and daughters than their dads spent with them. They are connecting earlier with their children and making real efforts to remain connected. They engage their kids more, listen to them, and hang out with them.

Marriages, as well, are getting better as couples work on them. More couples are going to marriage encounter weekends where they are learning more effective listening and communication skills. Couples are spending more time with each other also; many go out on dates every week. Dads are discovering that when they spend more time with their kids and are emotionally there for them, that their relationship with their wife improves. More couples, hopefully, are learning that marriage is a commitment that lasts a lifetime.

We are also learning something about what William Pollack calls the "boy code." Little boys do have feelings – they are sensitive, kind, and loving. Having these feelings doesn't turn them into sissies or mama's boys. The idea of the tough, independent, cool guy may be eroding. Moms and even many dads are not allowing coaches, scout leaders, camp directors and other leaders to continue the myth of the "boy code." We're also finding out that moms need to stay connected to their sons and that maternal instincts to do this are correct. Hugging and kissing – physical contact with boys doesn't turn them into wimps.

Boys need to be allowed to experience their feelings. They should be allowed to cry if they are hurt – it's natural for little boys to have feelings. For men to be sensitive, kind, and loving as husbands and fathers, they need to develop this behavior when they are young. We really can't have it both ways. The "boy code" hasn't worked very well for us as a culture – I hope that we will not allow this kind of thinking to continue, and that when we encounter it, we will have the courage to confront it.

Our priorities are also changing. Slowly, we are finding out that things aren't all that important. As priorities are discussed among couples, husbands are finding out that a bigger house or a new car is not really at the top of his wife's priority list. Wives want husbands home. Wives want husbands present emotionally and involved with the children. Even corporations are changing, e.g., giving time off for parents to be with their newborns. Corporations are learning that their employees are more productive when family concerns are regarded.

Schools have also gotten our attention. We are appalled by the violence. We are concerned about the safety of our own kids. This concern, hopefully, will show itself in more support for our public schools. Parents need to play a more active role in the education of their kids. There are many good schools with good teachers. Often, however, teachers feel overworked, underpaid and not appreciated. Thus, many good teachers are leaving the profession – this is a tragedy. We need good schoolteachers in our public school system and we need to pay them respectably.

Moreover, schools are changing. We are finding out that smaller schools and smaller classes are better. Some school districts are moving in that direction even though it costs more. Schools are also becoming safer places. Teachers and administrators are walking the halls and not tolerating taunting, guns, and other weapons. Many schools have developed relationships with police. Officers come to the schools on a regular basis. Their very presence has a calming effect on schools. Student crime stoppers programs are also being set up. Hot lines are available for students to report potentially dangerous situations before they happen. The police, in conjunction with school personnel, are developing plans of action in case an emergency does arise. Kids know when there is danger and who the dangerous kids are.

We are also learning how to spot troubled kids and becoming more aware that high school and middle school kids suffer from depression. These kids often become very angry. We're finding out that depression responds to medication. It can be treated. We are also more aware of ADHD and other learning disabilities in kids. These disabilities can be treated. As I read about the young men who were involved in the school shootings, I realize that many of them were emotionally troubled.

Over the years, we, as a culture, have developed a tolerance for violence. Movies, television, video games, and now the Internet all portray violence. Perhaps, we are getting to the point that we refuse to tolerate this pervasive violence. Maybe all this school violence has resensitized us to how very violent our culture is. Maybe the time is coming when we won't tolerate violent movies anymore, or make the actors who play in them national heroes.

Furthermore, I think we are becoming aware of how dangerous guns are and how easy it is for kids to get their hands on them. We need to enforce the laws that deal with gun control, but we need to have other laws that realistically ban assault weapons and keep guns out of the hands of kids. No one has the right to have guns that are produced just for the purpose of killing people.

Finally, there seems to be an increased awareness of the importance of God in our lives. Studies out of Cornell and Harvard show that kids who go to church or synagogues are less likely to be involved in drugs, alcohol, or sex than kids who don't attend places of worship are. The presence of God in our lives, at least as individuals, is gaining in importance. After the Littleton tragedy, 150 kids from Columbine High School showed up at the Young Life leader's home. High school kids all over the country are involved in Bible studies. More kids than ever are going to Young Life and church camps in the summer. Almost every college dormitory, sorority house, and fraternity house offer Bible studies. Kids are searching for meaning in their lives. Finding God makes sense to them. Kids who go to Bible studies, who pray, and who take God seriously usually don't shoot people.

I'm hopeful that things will change. I pray that our culture will become less violent. But, we are a lot like Cassie Bernall – we need conversion, radical transformation, turning around and going in a different direction. I agree with Nancy Gibbs, who wrote in her *Time* essay, "The Columbine tragedy didn't start out as a front-page story about the battle between good and evil. But it has been moving there...." If true, then all of us, like Cassie, need conversion.

Bibliography

"Annual Report on School Safety." U.S. Department of Education, 1998.

Chua-Eoan, Howard. *Escaping from the Darkness*. <u>Time</u> 31 May 1999: 44-49.

Cloud, John. *Just a Routine School Shooting*. <u>Time</u> 31 May 1999: 34-43.

Coles, Robert. *The Spiritual Life of Children*. Boston: Houghton Mifflin, 1990.

"Creating Safe and Drug-Free Schools: An Action Guide." U.S. Department of Education, 1999.

Elias, M. *Teens Do Better When Dads Are More Involved*. <u>U.S.A. Today.</u> 22 August 1996.

Erikson, Erik H. *Identity Youth and Crisis*. New York: W. W. Norton & Company, Inc., 1968.

Frankl, Viktor E. *Man's Search for Meaning*. New York: Washington Square Press, Inc., 1963.

Garbarino, James, Ph.D. *Lost Boys: why our sons turn violent and how we can save them*. New York: The Free Press, 1999.

Gibbs, Nancy. *Noon in the Garden of Good and Evil*. <u>Time</u>. 17 May 1999, 54.

Pollack, William, Ph.D. *Real Boys: rescuing our sons from the myths of boyhood.* New York: Henry Holt and Company, Inc., 1998.

Pooley, Eric. *Portrait of a Deadly Bond.* Time. 10 May 1999, 26-32.

Prothrow-Stith, Deborah, M.D. *Deadly Consequences: how violence is destroying our teenage population and a plan to begin solving the problem.* New York: HarperCollins Publishers, 1991.

Sharey, J. *How Fathers Care for the Next Generation: a four-decade study.* Cambridge: Harvard University Press, 1993.

"Teen Tips." The Times-Union. 30 August 1999, C-8.

Tournier, Paul. *The Violence Within.* New York: Harper & Row, 1977.

"What are they saying?" U.S. News & World Report. 3 May 1999, 21.

Index

Order Form
Publications & Videotapes by Herbert Wagemaker, M.D.

TITLE (Softcover Books)	Quantity	Cost	Total Cost
The Surprising Truth About Depression		$12 ea.	
Schizophrenia and Bipolar Disorders — often misdiagnosed, often mistreated: A Family Manual		$12 ea.	

VIDEOTAPE TITLE	Quantity	Cost	Total Cost
Schizophrenia		$10 ea.	
Bipolar Disorder		$10 ea.	
Depression		$10 ea.	
Adolescent Depression & Suicide		$10 ea.	
Postpartum Depression		$10 ea.	
Panic Disorder		$10 ea.	
Obsessive Compulsive Disorder		$10 ea.	
Attention Deficit Disorder & Hyperactivity		$10 ea.	
Learning Tapes - make learning fun/productive 1. elementary child 2. middle school age 3. high school age		$10 ea. $10 ea. $10 ea.	
Florida Residents add 6 1/2% for Sales Tax			
Shipping & Handling: $2/book & $2.50/videotape			
Total Amount Paid			

Shipping Address:
Name: _____
Address: _____
City: _____ State: _____ Zip: _____

Make checks payable to: **Ponte Vedra Publishers,
P.O. Box 773, Ponte Vedra Beach, FL 32004-0773**
Please allow 3 – 4 weeks for delivery.